IN THE PRESENCE OF GREATNESS

ISAIAH

MATT WILEY

DOUG SERVEN

White Blackbird
BOOKS

PRAISE FOR IN THE PRESENCE OF GREATNESS

Personal. Just the way Isaiah experienced it. When pastors give themselves to the craft of preaching and that to people in real time, the scene is holy. Doug Serven and Matt Wiley have shared those personal scenes in their book, *Isaiah: In the Presence of Greatness*. As a fellow pastor, I share their desire to see lives radically altered by fresh experiences of God's holiness. The promising news is that God includes us in his holiness through the not-so-ordinary experience of grace, his mercy wealth that affords us an impossibly close view. We are reminded how impossibly close as God meets us in local church communities week after week, Sabbath after Sabbath. You will be touched by the scenes. They are holy, because he is holy.

Brad Anderson
Pastor, Valley Springs Presbyterian Church

This book opens the complexity of Isaiah to pastors, as well as new and mature Christians, in a clear, but deep language. A gem that could be used as a tool for preachers, for any Christian, and for those seeking to explore Christianity.

Israel Ruiz
Pastor of Hispanic Ministries, Emmanuel Presbyterian Church

If you're like me, you know what it's like when your relationship with God simply isn't where you want it to be. I know because I'm a mess. In *Isaiah: In the Presence of Greatness*, Doug Serven and Matt Wiley bring you and your mess into the presence of a spiritual reality who is beyond terrifying . . . but who at the same time welcomes you with your mess because he's actually really, really into you. In the face of the tragedy of this life in a world of sorrows, you'll find renewed hope in the welcome of Jesus to sinners and mess-makers like us.

Greg Johnson
Pastor, Memorial Presbyterian Church

Isaiah is a mountain of a book and when you go to hike a giant mountain it is good to have a guide who is not only able to help you find your way but is able to see and enjoy the wonders you find along the way. Doug Serven and Matt Wiley give us not only helpful insights into what Isaiah was saying to his original audience but expose us to the rich and robust message Isaiah has for us in our present context as well. Both their biblical knowledge and pastoral experience make them excellent guides in not only gaining greater insight and understanding into what some have called the 5th gospel, but also enabling the reader to see the beauty and grace of God and how it applies in our present journey of faith. So whether you are a mom looking to be encouraged in the midst of the brokenness of family life, a husband needing to be reminded of how God has loved you in the midst of your struggles and doubts, or just a fellow traveler in the journey of faith looking for some seasoned and friendly guides, this is your book!

Dennis Hermerding
Pastor, King's Cross Church

CONTENTS

Introduction   ix

Isaiah 1   1
Isaiah 2   17
Isaiah 6   24
Isaiah 7, 9, 11   44
Isaiah 24–25   64
Isaiah 26   79
Isaiah 36–38   92
Isaiah 40   107
Isaiah 42–43   122
Isaiah 44   137
Isaiah 53–54   153
Isaiah 55   160
Isaiah 58, 61, 62   168
Isaiah 63–66   179

Notes   197
About White BlackBird Books   201
Also by White Blackbird Books   203

To the sinner-saints at City Presbyterian Church in Oklahoma City who heard these sermons. And to the sinner-saints at Shawnee Presbyterian Church, the church that was started soon after we did this series.

May the Lord bless and keep you. May he make his face to shine upon you and be gracious unto you. May he lift up his countenance up you and give you peace.

INTRODUCTION

The towering promises made in the book of Isaiah loom large for Old Testament characters, New Testament writers, and early church fathers. This majestic literature shows God's repeated pattern and plan of bringing reconciliation and justice, his faithfulness in making all things right. For centuries, people have read about Isaiah's Suffering Servant, the promised redeemer.

In the summer of 2017 after I (Matt) was ordained to pastoral ministry, Doug Serven and I found hope and comfort as we preached from Isaiah at City Presbyterian Church in Oklahoma City.

The book of Isaiah does not come out of nowhere. It is an integral part of God's unfolding narrative of redemption. At the beginning of the Bible, we read about how God made everything good. In fact it was not *just* good. After God had finished creating everything, he pronounced it *very* good. Everything was good and right in the world. Humanity was in perfect relationship with God, with one another, and with creation.

But peace and harmony came to an end. Humanity questioned God's goodness and, rather than trust God, it looked to other sources of wisdom and rebelled against God. This disobedience plunged the world into sin, misery, and alienation. As a result of this rebellion, humanity was alienated from God, one another, and creation.

The good news is God did not leave humanity, but he pursued us despite our brokenness and shame, and he promised to make things right. God promised that someone would come to bring deliverance and restoration.

As the Bible continues to unfold God's story, we see him at work to bring this restoration through a man named Abraham. God tells Abraham to go to a new land, and God will make him into a great nation. They will be a numerous people, they will have land, and they will bring blessings to all the nations and to all the families of the earth. God has been their God, and he will continue to be their God despite their rebellion. God will bring restoration.

This is a key theme in the book of Isaiah—how God will bring about restoration and his people to himself. God is the Holy One of Israel, and he is creating a holy place and a holy people among whom he will dwell forever.

One of the questions addressed throughout our study is, "What does it look like to be in the presence of greatness?" In Isaiah 6 we get a picture of what it looks like for Isaiah to catch a glimpse of the holiness of God. We are told Isaiah sees the Lord sitting upon his throne, high and lifted up, with the train of his robe filling the temple. It is an awesome scene. Creatures known as seraphim are flying around calling out to one another, *"Holy, holy, holy is the LORD of hosts; the whole earth is full of his glory!"* (Isa. 6:3). Isaiah feels the foundations of the temple begin to shake. Isaiah recognizes he is not just in the presence of greatness but of pure holiness. How terrifying!

When Isaiah is confronted with this holiness, he also sees his sin. He cries out, *"Woe is me! For I am lost; for I am a man of unclean lips and I dwell in the midst of a people of unclean lips; for my eyes have seen the King, the LORD of hosts!"* (6:5). Isaiah recognizes he is a sinner, and he needs cleansing. He knows he is lost and needs salvation.

This is not just a problem for Isaiah but also for the nation of Israel. God had promised them he would be their God, and they would be his people. Israel had failed to live as God's people. They rejected his word and failed to be a light to the nations. No amount of judgment, deliverance from enemies, or repentance would change Israel. Instead of letting God's story shape their lives, God's people believed the narrative of the world.

This is not just a problem for Israel but also for all humanity. The bad news is we cannot change or purify ourselves. Only God can save, and only God can purify. He is going to do what we cannot. He is going to purify us by making atonement for our sins and making all things new and right.

The good news for Isaiah is he is not left in his sin and impurity. God enters in and provides purification and cleansing for Isaiah. This man who said his lips were unclean has his lips purified. He writes:

> *Then one of the seraphim flew to me, having in his hand a burning coal that he had taken with tongs from the altar. And he touched my mouth and said: "Behold this has touched your lips; your gilt is taken away and your sin atoned for." (6:6–7)*

Not only is Isaiah forgiven, but he is commissioned to go and tell this message of justice and grace to a people who don't want to hear it. Israel fails to understand the grace it receives in being the children of God. They are a people of unclean lips. They live lives of wickedness, oppression, and violence. Justice and righteousness are the results from God's purifying grace, and only through receiving and understanding grace will God's people change. Ultimately, purifying grace will change the universe.

Isaiah calls the nation of Israel to repent and let God's story of grace shape their lives. Isaiah retells God's promise to provide one who will bring our needed salvation. Isaiah speaks of one who will come as a Suffering Servant. This servant will come and live the life we cannot live and die the death we deserve to die. Isaiah tells us, *"All we like sheep have gone astray; we have turned everyone to his own way; and the LORD has laid on him the iniquity of us all"* (53:6). Israel could not earn its salvation and neither can we. But God will provide one who dies in the place of his people. He will pay the penalty for our sins.

This salvation is bigger than just forgiveness of sins.

Imagine you bounced a check at your bank. You spent money you did not have in your account. Your bank will not cover the cost of anything you don't have in your account, and they will charge you an additional fee for writing a check your account could not cover. You now owe a debt to your bank. If the bank decides to cancel the debt you owe and forgive the cost of your debts, that is good news! The problem is that after those debts are forgiven, you still have nothing in your account. That is not good news, but Isaiah shows us a better salvation.

Salvation is bigger than the personal forgiveness of sins. God provides a lavish welcome into his presence. This is the story of the Bible—God is the great welcomer. He invites us to feast at his table. It is all his grace. God welcomes straying sinners to his feast. Isaiah writes, *"Come, everyone who thirsts, come to the waters; and he who has no money come, buy and eat! Come, buy wine and milk without money and without price"* (55:1).

God provides salvation by his grace. It is a lavish salvation that welcomes and provides. God's salvation does not just provide the forgiveness of sins but also gives the lavish welcome of God. We are given the sustenance and nourishment we so desperately need. God has sent a Savior who not only forgives us of our sins, but also lavishes and blesses us with every spiritual blessing.

Isaiah also shows us how God provides reconciliation for all things. When Jesus, the promised Savior Isaiah points to, comes on the scene, one of the first things he does is read from Isaiah. He says:

> *The Spirit of the Lord is upon me, because he has anointed me to proclaim good news to the poor. He has sent me to proclaim liberty to the captives and recovering of sight to the blind, to set at liberty those who are oppressed, to proclaim the year of the Lord's favor.* (Luke 4:18–19)

This salvation Isaiah looks to and Jesus inaugurates is not just a spiritual salvation. It has real impacts in the here and now of the world we live in. God is not just reconciling individuals to himself. He's saving the whole universe.

Yes, humanity is reconciled to God through Jesus, but salvation is bigger than that. People are also reunited to one another. Isaiah had tasted the purification and reconciliation of God, and he was sent to proclaim this message to Israel and all people. We can be one with God, one another, and all things. One day, all the effects of man's rebellion will be reversed because God is faithful to his promises. One day, all things will be made new and right.

This is the good news Isaiah proclaims. Isaiah points us to God's great story of redemption. It shows us our need, and it points us to a reconciliation far bigger and greater than we could imagine. It reminds us we can't do anything to earn any of this.

God has done it all. He has sent his servant to live the life we could not live and die the death we deserve to die. God's son Jesus Christ has brought the salvation we all long for.

ISAIAH 1

What do you do when you get in the presence of greatness? How do you feel when you stand in front of something incredible and amazing? What's your reaction when you finally get to meet the person you've always admired and patterned your life after?

I (Doug) remember the first time I took my kids to the Grand Canyon. My friend Russ flew out from Virginia for his Spring Break when he was teaching high school English to go with me. My youngest daughter Anna was only about four at the time, so the fourteen-hour drive out there was not fun. Russ had to grade papers, so he was preoccupied. The kids spilled chips and goldfish crackers all over the car. We stayed in a pretty dumpy hotel to save money.

Was this perhaps the worst decision I'd made in a long time? The kids were not fired up to see a huge hole in the ground. They wanted rides, movies, and fun. They didn't know what we were about to see, and I couldn't explain it to them.

I was not delivering.

Then we walked out to the vista, and it took my breath away. Theirs too (for five minutes).

Have you been to the Grand Canyon? Have you stepped out and seen that view? It's glorious, tremendous. There is nothing quite like it.

It made me feel small. It made me feel quieter inside, calmed. It made me feel somewhat nervous, as I didn't want to make the trip home with some of my kids missing at the bottom of the canyon. It was strangely both peaceful and unsettling at the same time.

We're going to be thinking about Grand-Canyon-type greatness as we work through the ancient book of Isaiah.

———

I've always loved the book of Isaiah. It has so many great memorizable passages and memorable images. Isaiah is the Shakespeare of the Old Testament because Isaiah changes literature. He is quoted in the New Testament sixty-six times, more times than all of the other Old Testament prophets added together.

I've loved Isaiah, but I haven't always understood it. Once you put the cool sound bites in their context, you realize this is a huge book. It has a ton of chapters. It's mostly written in poetry, but it has some crazy history stuck in the middle. You start to scratch your head and wonder what it all means.

We may not necessarily answer all your questions in this book. We won't cover every verse of Isaiah line by line (you wouldn't be able to pay attention that long!). As we work through this great book, we hope you'll be thinking about a lot of things, but ultimately it should be about Jesus Christ and your relationship to him.

Let's look at a few introductory points to get ourselves oriented to Isaiah. Isaiah 1:1 will help us gain our bearings: *"The vision of Isaiah the son of Amoz, which he saw concerning Judah and Jerusalem in the days of Uzziah, Jotham, Ahaz, and Hezekiah, kings of Judah."*

Vision

The first word we encounter in this book (after "the") is "vision." Isaiah received a vision from God, which he passed on to God's people, and this is what we read today.

Christians believe God actually spoke his words through certain people. These authors didn't go into trances or somehow channel God. They retained their personality and personhood while at the same time writing the very words of God. This isn't a popular idea in postmodern or academic settings. Your response to the idea that God could do this will not only affect your reading of this book but your view on life as a whole.

All of us believe in prophets at some level. You read articles from people predicting who will win the Oscars. Often they have columns discussing "Who should win" and "Who will win." Preview magazines for college football or the NFL are huge businesses. People scour reports on who will be the next prospect or president or Kentucky Derby winner.

What about the weather? Meteorologists give you a ten-day forecast. Do you believe them? Do you pack your umbrella when it's rainy or watch when there is a tornado warning?

The idea of prophets is not foreign to us after all. We need them, and we listen to them.

Here are four biblical affirmations about prophets:

1. The prophets considered themselves servants of God, vehicles through whom himself spoke.
2. They considered the content of their message unoriginal.
3. They considered themselves as occupying a divinely appointed societal office, correcting illegal beliefs and practices.
4. They understood what they preached in a qualified way.

Deuteronomy 18:15–22 will help you understand God's prophets. We read:

> The LORD your God will raise up for you a prophet like me from among you, from your brothers–it is to him you shall listen–just as you desired of the LORD your God at Horeb on the day of the assembly, when you said, "Let me not hear again the voice of the LORD my God or see this great fire any more, lest I die." And the LORD said to me, "They are right in what they have spoken. I will raise up for them a prophet like you from among their brothers. And I will put my words in his mouth, and he shall speak to them all that I command him. And whoever will not listen to my words that he shall speak in my name, I myself will require it of him. But the prophet who presumes to speak a word in my name that I have not commanded him to speak, or who speaks in the name of other gods, that same prophet shall die." And if you say in your heart, "How may we know

the word that the LORD has not spoken?" when a prophet speaks in the name of
the LORD, if the word does not come to pass or come true, that is a word that the
LORD has not spoken; the prophet has spoken it presumptuously. You need not
be afraid of him.

I could say a lot about this, and it would make an interesting seminary class. It could easily fill a whole year's worth of preaching and teaching.

But in order to keep it short and sweet, I want you to know you can have confidence in Isaiah as the Word of God, as God speaking to you. God himself set up certain rules for judging prophets in a world of competing voices. There were other talking heads out there, other prophecies. God knew this, and he spoke about it. He says you have to watch and see who was telling the truth and what proved to come true.

If someone gets her sports predictions wrong every time, we should stop listening to her. If someone never picks the Oscars right, we need a new columnist. If someone cannot get the weather accurately, we hire him for a big contract—but we shouldn't.

The same was true for prophets. Isaiah has a ton of unfulfilled prophecies when he spoke them, but he met the qualifications for prophet set out in Deuteronomy. That didn't necessarily do the people of Isaiah's time any good, since the fulfillment came too late for them to adequately check him out.

Dr. Craige illuminates this for us when he writes:

It would probably be wrong to take these criteria as rules to be applied rigidly every time a prophet opened his mouth. When a prophet announced God's coming judgment and called for repentance, it would clearly be pointless to wait first to see if the judgment actually came to pass, and then to repent (too late!). Rather the criteria represent the means by which a prophet gained his reputation as a true prophet and spokesman of the Lord. Over the course of a prophet's ministry, in matters important and less significant, the character of a prophet as a true spokesman of God would begin to emerge clearly. And equally, false prophets would be discredited and then dealt with under the law.[1]

Patrick Fairbairn was a Scottish pastor from the nineteenth century. He teaches us:

> The prophet, as regarded in light of the Scripture, was simply the recipient and bearer of a message from God; and such a message of course was prophecy, whatever might be its more specific character— whether the disclosure of some important truth, the inculcation of an imperative duty, or a prospective delineation of coming events.[2]

What do you think? Were there prophets? Did God really speak, or are these the collected speeches and writings of people who knew God and were really smart and eloquent, or part of a winning faction who rewrote history to their benefit?

If God hasn't spoken to us, then how do you orient yourself toward the world? Is there a beginning and an end to human history on the earth? If not, then why is this current moment significant? Why do you matter if this is a huge, cosmic evolutionary tale?

Remember, prophets are a popular way to communicate. Who helped Neo in *The Matrix*? Was it strange for there to be an Oracle to consult in times of trouble, someone who saw the future even though she didn't know exactly how it would be fulfilled?

Remember the prophecy in *Star Wars*? Someone would come, someone who had tremendous ability and power, who would bring balance to the Force. That prophecy guided many of the actions of the characters.

And so it might be true for us today. You might consider that if there is a God, he could speak through his prophets, and they could likewise still speak to us.

Christianity contends that God himself became a man. He was born of a virgin. He did miracles. And, after dying on a cross, he rose from the dead. Then he ascended to heaven, where he reigns and will come back someday. Not to mention God created the universe by the word of his power in the space of six days, and it was all very good.

So God being able to speak through prophets actually seems like pretty tame stuff for a God who does all those mind-boggling activities.

Isaiah

The next word we get to is "Isaiah." *"Isaiah, son of Amoz"* (Isa. 1:1).

Who is Isaiah, and is he really the author of this book? If you take a class at a university, (or many seminaries) you might get the modern theory—Isaiah didn't write the book that bears his name. He may have written the first part, chapters 1–39, but the tone of the book changes so much there had to be a second author and maybe even a third. Or an "Isaiah school" listened, learned, and wrote like their master.

Why this authorship idea? Why not take the attribution at face value?

Credit for developing a full-blown theory of various authors is usually given to J. C. Doderlein (1775) and J. G. Eichhorn (1780–83) for three main reasons:

1. The historical setting of chapters 40–66 reflect the exilic period because Jerusalem is depicted as having fallen and been deported.
2. The striking difference in language, style and concepts between the two parts of the book point to different authors.
3. The Hebrew prophet was, the theory holds, primarily given a message for his own day and chapters 40–66 are said not to be addressed to people of the eighth century.

The current, modern theory is Isaiah is to be read in three distinct parts: Isaiah I, 1–39; Isaiah II, 40–55; Isaiah III, 56–66.

One of the driving forces in this is the *impossibility* for someone to know what is going to happen in the future. That just doesn't happen in the normal course of life.

So they say it *cannot* happen. If Isaiah writes in the 700s BC, then when we start to read about Cyrus in the 500s BC, we obviously have a different writer. This thought and philosophy doesn't believe God could actually speak through a prophet and speak into the future.

The response to this has been generally along three lines:

1. The present literary context attributes the whole book to Isaiah, and Jewish tradition and New Testament authority support this.

2. There are enough similarities in language and concepts to maintain a single authorship. Differences can be explained by new subject matter, altered intention, and a later date in the life of the prophet (time passed between when he started and when he finished).

3. The supernatural quality of the prophecy is jeopardized if chapters 40–66 were written in the sixth century or later, rather than in the eighth century or early eighth (does a prophet have supernatural knowledge of the future [if God chooses to give it] or not?)[3]

Commentator J. Alec Motyer writes:

The most natural way of taking the superscription in 1:1 (which refers to Isaiah in the third person) is that it is from the hand of the final editor, who wishes to affirm that the book as a whole is a faithful expression of the vision (revelation) which was given to Isaiah. From the editor's own point of view, the period of the prophet's life is past. It was *"in the days of Jotham, Ahaz and Hezekiah, kings of Judah"* that the vision came. A similar backward look occurs in the third person accounts of events in Isaiah's life in chapters 20 and 36–39. These are quite different in style and viewpoint from the autobiographical material in chapters 6–8. In the present arrangement of the book, Isaiah's account of his call does not occur until chapter 6. It is preceded by material that has apparently been placed before it for thematic reasons, some of it drawn from quite late in his ministry. There is clear evidence of editorial activity in the production of the present book, and it makes good sense to attribute this to Isaiah's disciples.[4]

We believe Isaiah wrote this book.

There has been an academic renewal toward viewing the book in its unity, not separating it into parts. Isaiah may have written it as he preached and heard from God over his lifetime and, when he had died, some editors may have put it together thematically instead of chronologically. If Isaiah truly spoke with God, Isaiah would be able to know, if God revealed it to him, the name of King Cyrus two-hundred years in the future—after all, that is a part of the nature of what validates the ministry of a true prophet.

One more important thing to note before we move on—Isaiah's name means "Yahweh's salvation." The Hebrew words for "he shall save" and "salvation" are forms of this name, Isaiah. God is issuing and ushering his salvation through Isaiah the prophet. It might not be surprising that one bearing that name would speak of amazing things of God, things revealed by God himself.

History

The last thing we need to know before we begin is the historical context. Isaiah (or most likely the editor who compiled Isaiah's writings) writes, *"which he saw concerning Judah and Jerusalem in the days of Uzziah, Jotham, Ahaz, and Hezekiah, kings of Judah"* (1:1).

Chapters 1–39

Uzziah was the King of Judah, the southern kingdom (Israel had been split into two kingdoms, Israel and Judah, around 930 BC, see 1 Kings 12), during the first half of the eighth century BC. During Uzziah's reign, Israel (the northern kingdom) and Judah enjoyed a golden age of prosperity. God's people stood in the path between the day's superpowers: Assyria, Damascus, and Babylon to the north and Egypt to the south. But Egypt was weak and all Assyria could manage was to keep Damascus too off-kilter to bother Israel.

However, things began to change. Five years before Uzziah's death, a new ruler came to power in Assyria (Tiglath-Pileser III), and he quickly took over Babylon, secured his northern border, and began to take over the lands to the south. He took the Syrian city of Arpad, and so Damascus, Israel, and Tyre began paying tribute hoping to avoid an invasion, which was a common, though risky, practice in the Ancient Near East.

Thus, when Uzziah died, Assyria went on the move, and there was no one to stop their advance into Judah. Things looked grim. Powerful Assyria was on Jerusalem's doorstep. Besides this external threat, there were internal problems. Justice was being bought and sold, and religion had become an outward show with no reality underneath. Before Uzziah's death, Israel and Damascus formed a defensive alliance and tried to persuade Judah to join. Judah refused, so Israel and Damascus attacked Judah (with Ahaz as the king of Judah now). Things looked bad for Judah, but Isaiah told Ahaz to stand firm and trust God. Instead, Ahaz appealed to Assyria for help. This made Judah a slave state to Assyria. Eventually Israel and Damascus were wiped out by Assyria, and Judah struggled to survive under the cruel Assyrian yoke.

When Hezekiah became King of Judah, he decided his kingdom could no longer live under Assyrian control, so he organized a coalition to revolt (which includes Babylon to Assyria's north). But Assyria (with Sennacherib as their king) proved stronger than anyone predicted and crushed Babylon. Now they could turn their full attention toward Judah. Judah looked to Egypt for help, but they too proved ineffective.

All of Judea is wiped out except Jerusalem (which is saved by a miraculous intervention by God, second only to the Exodus as God's great deliverance of his people in the Old Testament).

Chapters 40–66

Most of Isaiah 1–39 relates to the crisis described above. But within five years after God's deliverance of Jerusalem from the hands of Sennacherib of Assyria, Manasseh (one of the worst kings of Judah) had plunged Judah into one of its darkest periods. He brought Judah under the complete control of Assyria and introduced all sorts of pagan idolatry. According to tradition, Isaiah was martyred during this time by being put into a hollow log and sawn in two! But during this dark period, God revealed more fully to Isaiah the glorious hope of return from exile (fulfilled in the 500s

BC) and the future work of the Messiah and his kingdom that will have no end.[5]

Jesus

John writes about an important moment in Jesus' ministry:

> When Jesus had said these things, he departed and hid himself from them. Though he had done so many signs before them, they still did not believe in him, so that the word spoken by the prophet Isaiah might be fulfilled: "Lord, who has believed what he heard from us, and to whom has the arm of the Lord been revealed?" Therefore they could not believe. For again Isaiah said, "He has blinded their eyes, and hardened their heart, lest they see with their eyes, and understand with their heart, and turn, and I would heal them."
>
> Isaiah said these things because he saw his glory and spoke of him. Nevertheless, many even of the authorities believed in him, but for fear of the Pharisees they did not confess it, so that they would not be put out of the synagogue; for they loved the glory that comes from man more than the glory that comes from God.
>
> And Jesus cried out and said, "Whoever believes in me, believes not in me but in him who sent me. And whoever sees me sees him who sent me. I have come into the world as light, so that whoever believes in me may not remain in darkness. If anyone hears my words and does not keep them, I do not judge him; for I did not come to judge the world but to save the world. The one who rejects me and does not receive my words has a judge; the word that I have spoken will judge him on the last day. For I have not spoken on my own authority, but the Father who sent me has himself given me a commandment—what to say and what to speak. And I know that his commandment is eternal life. What I say, therefore, I say as the Father has told me." (John 12:36–50)

We have to end with Jesus. It's great and important to learn about prophets, for that helps us to believe this book can be the very words of God. We need to understand what God has spoken. It's good to know about Isaiah, for he was the prophet God chose at this time and place to give us these words. It's good to discover the historical context, so we can better understand the situation of the time and how we can apply it to our day.

But we could walk away with full heads and big brains and yet not have changed at all. It happens all the time. We learn, but we don't change. We study, but we aren't transformed.

The New Testament apostle and gospel writer John uses Isaiah's words in John 12 to say this very thing. John believed Isaiah. He quotes Isaiah with a working knowledge. He knew these words, and he could use and apply them.

In John 12, Jesus says there is a blindness for the people, a hardening of their hearts. They know these things. They have heard *about* Jesus. They've seen Jesus. He's walked among them. They have firsthand evidence, but they will not believe. They will not submit to or bow the knee to him. They make excuses for what they see and hear. There always must be another response than loving and following Jesus.

Are you blind? Do you think you see but in fact you can't? Jesus says if you think you can see, you are mistaken. But if you admit you are blind, you can finally see.

Hm.

In this passage in John and in this book of Isaiah, we're not going to tell you how wonderful you are. We're not going to tell you you're just almost there, you've almost got it, or there are just a few tweaks here and there you should make.

Isaiah starts his book off with the bad news:

Hear, O heavens and give ear, O earth; for the Lord has spoken; "Children I have reared and brought up, but they have rebelled against me. The ox knows its owner, and the donkey its master's crib, but Israel does not know, my people do not understand." (1:2–3)

He keeps going:

Ah, sinful nation, a people laden with iniquity, offspring of evildoers, children who deal corruptly! They have forsaken the Lord, they have despised the Holy One of Israel, they are utterly estranged. (1:4)

We're going to tell you—you stink. You are really, really awful, more than you and anyone else realizes. We're sorry, but that's the reality of the situation and to tell you differently would be dishonest.

We'd all like to hire a personal trainer and after our first consultation, she says, "I'm sorry, but I can't help you. You're in too good of shape. Your fat content is practically zero. Your nutrition is fantastic. Your posture is perfect. In fact, could you train me?"

We'd like to get assessed with A+, 110 percent, 20/20, and gold stars and medals all around. No one can stop you! You're the standard for perfection in performance and attitude. You have the heart of a champion.

Then—we wake up from that dream.

We know the reality of what we'll hear, so we avoid any type of assessment at all. If I'm unhealthy, then my natural tendency is to hang around other unhealthy people so I can go unnoticed. I don't want to have to change, so I normalize my dysfunction.

Isaiah calls you out!

You wandered out of the fast food and into the healthy eating section. You wandered off the couch and into the 5k! You joined a CrossFit gym on accident!

First, hear that where you are is not a good place. Listen.

It's not true that you have 20/20, 20/40 or 20/50 vision. You are blind. It's worse than you thought.

It's not that you're a bit out of shape. Your arteries are clogged. You can't keep going this way!

You're not earning 110 percent. It's more like one percent, if that.

You are hard-hearted. You do your own thing, think your own way, rule your own life. You sin all the time.

So do I. Then, not only do I sin, but I hide my sin so others won't find out. So then I'm a sinner, and I'm also a liar and a hider.

And it keeps getting worse.

This is the bad news. You will have to see yourself in this book as a worse person than you have thought. It's going to take an honest look at your life, one that will not present a pretty picture. Are you ready?

Or will you keep hiding, keep pretending to see because you don't want to get help? Keep lying?

Although he's a prophet of judgment, Isaiah speaks words of

hope right from the beginning. If you took to heart the bad news, then perk up at the good news:

> *Wash yourselves; make yourselves clean; removed the evil of your deeds from before my eyes; cease to do evil, learn to do good; seek justice; correct oppression; bring justice to the fatherless, plead the widow's case. Come, let us reason together, says the Lord; though your sins are like scarlet, they shall be as white as snow; though they are red like crimson, they shall become like wool.* (Isa. 1:16–18)

There is a blindness, a stink, a death. You may have come by it naturally or honestly. You have been born into it (in a sense, we all were). You may have chosen it. You may not have known any better.

But today, there can be a new day. A rooster crows to let you know the darkness can be over and the sunlight can burst through.

Jesus saves sinners like you and me. He cleanses us and makes us clean. He removes evil from our hands and hearts.

One of my friends recently relayed a story about how a friend of his became a millionaire. He said the secret of his success wasn't hard work, or luck, or good timing. He said he became a millionaire by spending time with other millionaires.

We don't work to make ourselves clean. We spend time with Jesus, who makes us clean. We don't work to make ourselves righteous. Jesus' righteousness is applied to us, and we walk in it. If we truly walk with him, he will lead us to other places than we normally go—into justice, goodness, correcting oppression, loving the fatherless, and helping widows.

He tells us we have work to do, and then as we spend time with him united by faith to him, we see our lives and hearts change. We see people and the world differently with his eyes and heart. We begin to understand sacrificial, suffering love. We begin to become one with him and thus united to others. Our hearts break, but they're also restored and given hope as we see the change only Jesus brings!

Jesus embraces, affirms, and then fulfills Isaiah's words. He is the light of the world, and in him there is no darkness. There may be dark places in your life and heart, but he will heal. He doesn't flash his 1000-watt floodlight immediately, but he may startle you by going into a room you thought you had successfully hidden and sealed. He'll find a way to get in there to bring light. He'll spray Lysol to let out the ghosts and demons that live there.

That room is there for a reason, but it can be redeemed and restored in Jesus. He's come to set the captives free. He gives hope. He has the authority given him by the Father to banish the evil and call in the good.

All this means there is hope. We live in a dark world, and we ourselves have dark hearts. We clamor around the darkness pretending we can see so we won't be exposed. Jesus invites us to come out of the darkness, out of the blindness, and into the glorious light of the Gospel.

There's hope that we might walk with Jesus and see the light. Evil will be defeated—we have a resurrection hope for this!

We might learn to do some good along the way. There might be justice in our city, state, nation, and world. Oppression might be corrected. Orphans can be cared and advocated for, and widows' cases might be heard so they can get care, roofs, lawns mowed, food, and have adopted children and grandchildren all around them. Single moms can have families rally around them, read to their kids, have good healthcare, and jobs where they make enough to live in big and safe enough homes. Kids might learn to read in schools that aren't overcrowded, with art and music classes, and high achievement with diversity, and they wouldn't go home hungry over the weekends or summers. Our justice system might be just after all. We might severely limit—not expand—evil payday loans. Our politicians could be held accountable and even forgiven when need be.

James Baldwin wrote, "Not everything that is faced can be changed. But nothing can be changed until it is faced."[6]

Jesus' greatness means there is hope for our souls and our world!

There's hope for you in the suburbs, the city, your apartment, and in your room.

There's hope for you in your marriage, in your singleness, in your divorce, in your loneliness, and in the weeds of widowhood.

There's hope for you behind the register, pushing a broom, cleaning toilets, changing gauze, crunching numbers, staying at home, in kindergarten, all the way up to high school, college, grad school, and med school graduation.

There's hope when you're at the end of your rope, sick and tired, exhausted, and when there doesn't look like there's a way out. There's hope when you got the promotion, grade, the ask, the engagement, or the ultrasound—or didn't.

Let's face it and ask Jesus to change it. May he redeem by justice and give us his righteousness as we repent. When we are weak, he is strong.

At the end of my run as the Reformed University Fellowship (RUF) campus minister at the University of Oklahoma, my intern Natalie got to meet one of her heroes—the Pioneer Woman, Ree Drummond. She spoke at OU, so Natalie blocked off her day, packed her cookbook, and started stalking her.

I talked to Natalie several times that afternoon, and she was always pretty unsure of herself. Should she talk to Ree? Should she approach her? She's so amazing and awesome! Being on the same campus as the Pioneer Woman made Natalie both thrilled and nervous (and I had a good time threatening to fire her if she didn't show up to our staff meeting at our allotted time because I knew where Natalie was).

We get thrilled and nervous when we get around someone we respect and admire. We so want to meet her and be around her, but there is something unsettled in our hearts.

Natalie did approach the Pioneer Woman, and she got her autograph. What do you think the Pioneer Woman was like?

She's important, busy, famous, and big-time. But she is also gracious and kind, and she spoke kind words to Natalie and said she was honored to meet her.

I hesitate to say Jesus is our Pioneer Woman, but in this illustration—he is. He is The Greater Pioneer Woman. He is busier, famouser, and more important. And he makes us feel unsettled. When you get around him, you may lose your bearings. In fact, you should. He should throw you off. You should not just have the same normal day, the same normal life, the same normal heart. He is so great, big, deep, majestic, and so mighty.

He's also kind, inviting, and the light to your dark soul. Jesus saves.

————

Sometimes a light surprises the Christian while he sings;
It is the Lord who rises with healing in His wings:
When comforts are declining, He grants the soul again
a season of clear shining, to cheer it after the rain.

In holy contemplation we sweetly then pursue
the theme of God's salvation, and find it ever new;
Set free from present sorrow, we cheerfully can say,
Let the unknown tomorrow bring with it what it may.

Tomorrow can bring us nothing, but He will bear us through:
Who gives the lilies clothing will clothe His people, too:
Beneath the spreading heavens no creature but is fed;
And He who feeds the ravens will give His children bread.

Though vine nor fig tree neither their wonted fruit should bear,
though all the fields should wither, Nor flocks or herds be there .
Yet, God the same abiding, His praise shall tune my voice;
For, while in Him confiding, I cannot but rejoice.[7]

ISAIAH 2

I (Matt) need Isaiah 2.

In one week, I attended two funerals, and our beloved dog died. I was constantly reminded we live in a broken world. I was confronted with the sting of death and the struggles of addiction and brokenness.

Right after I found out I passed my ordination exams on the floor of presbytery, I received a call saying my uncle had only a few hours left to live. I was able to see him and tell him how much I loved him and how I appreciated that he pointed me to Jesus.

His last words to me were, "Hold on to the Word of God, because that is all that you have." They are words I will never forget, ones I will cling to for the rest of my life.

Isaiah 2:5 is something I hold to during difficult weeks: *"O house of Jacob, come, let us walk in the light of the LORD."* I need light—we all do—because light not only exposes darkness in our lives, but light shows us the way forward and is a source of hope. So as we look at this passage I want to highlight three things: false hopes, Gospel hope, and the mission of hope.

False Hopes

Where do we find hope?

What is the anchor of your soul? Where do you find value and meaning? What do you look to for hope?

I love what we see in verse 2. Isaiah writes:

> It shall come to pass in the latter days that the mountain of the LORD shall be established as the highest of the mountains, and shall be lifted up above the hills and all the nations shall flow to it. (Isa. 2:2)

In the ancient world, all the gods were thought to dwell on mountains. Zeus dwelled on Mount Olympus. Pagan gods were worshipped on high places.

The people of Judah worshipped God on a mountain too. The temple was built on Mt. Zion. In verse 2, we read that one day God will shine forth as the one true God who created all things. The one true God is faithful to all his promises, and we hope in him.

This picture of the nations flowing to the mountain of the Lord calls us back to the promise God made to Abraham back in Genesis 12 when he says, *"In you all the families of the earth shall be blessed"* (Gen. 12:3).

God blessed Abraham and made him into a great nation, one where God would be their God, and they would be his people. But as the biblical story unfolds, it goes another way. Israel fails to follow God. They don't let his promises shape their lives. They put their hope in other things.

We read in Isaiah 2:6–8:

> For you have rejected your people the house of Jacob because they are full of things from the east and of fortune tellers like the Philistines, and they strike hands with the children of foreigners. Their land is full of silver and gold, and there is no end to their treasures, their land is filled with horses and there is no end to their chariots. Their land is filled with idols; they bow down to the works of their hands, to what their own fingers have made.

Instead of finding hope in the God of Jacob, they look to the gods of the other nations. They make alliances with other nations, and they amass wealth and strength for themselves. Instead of looking to God to bless them, they look to the nations around them. They worship their false gods, putting their hope and trust in them. And instead of blessing others, they consume things from the nations around them.

God's people had a call to be like bacon. Even though they couldn't eat it (because of the dietary laws), they were to be like this delicious meat.

How do you make any food better? You add bacon to it. Bacon makes everything taste amazing. Bacon enhances the flavor of food with its salty, porky goodness.

Now compare bacon with something like tofu. Tofu doesn't taste like anything. When you put tofu into food, it absorbs the flavors around it.

Judah was called to be a flavoring agent in the world (like bacon). Instead (like tofu), they absorbed the idols and values of the world.

Judah looked to other things to give them hope. They were consumers.

This is what it looks like to be a consumer instead of a worshipper of God. They were looking to manipulate God to get what they wanted in life. If God was not doing what they wanted, they gave themselves to other things they thought would give meaning, purpose, and hope in life.

We do the same thing. We look to other things to give us hope. We center our lives around something else to find purpose and meaning.

One of the places we look for hope is in ourselves, or at least I do.

Recently, Doug spoke to me as we came to the Lord's Supper. I'm grateful for his words to me. It was right before the time in our worship service where I was to be ordained as a pastor and church planter, and he reminded me the table is not about me. It is not about my accomplishments.

I needed to hear those words, because it is easy to look to myself for strength and hope. When I started a church in Shawnee, it was easy to rely on my own strengths and my own efforts. But if I bank on my own abilities, I will fail.

This is what was going on in Judah. They were relying on their own strength.

Under Uzziah's reign, everything seemed to be going well for them. They had amassed large amounts of silver and gold. They had chariots and horses. Uzziah's name means "the Lord is my strength," but instead of relying on the Lord, success and wealth led Uzziah to believe "I am my own strength."

Putting our hope in ourselves and relying on our own strength won't work. It's a false hope. Verse 12 says, *"For the LORD of hosts has a day against all that is proud and lofty, against all that is lifted up—and it shall be brought low"* (Isa. 2:12). As a pastor, if I try to look good, if I find my value in our awesome building, or if I find my hope in the number of people who attend my church—it won't work.

The problem for Judah, and for us, is we put our hope in ourselves, or we put our hope in the things of this world. We look to ourselves for our worth and value. We look for hope in what we make, in what we achieve, or in what we do. Or we look for hope in our kids, in what they make, in what they achieve, and in what they do.

I talked to a dad whose six-year-old son was outside swinging around a broomstick. He was hoping to increase the speed of his son's swing. He said, "I think this will help my son make it to the big leagues."

I wasn't sure if this was a goal for hockey or baseball, but either way it is the hope of pride. It leads us to go out and find significance for ourselves. It is a false hope, and it will leave us empty. It will bring us low. Look at 2:11:

The haughty looks of man shall be brought low, and the lofty pride of men shall be humbled, and the LORD alone will be exalted on that day.

If you read chapter 2, you will see over and over again the pride of man brought low.

The Hope of the Gospel

The good news (the Gospel) is that there is a hope.

There is a hope that will not leave us empty. There is a place where you can find hope and significance, and it is only in Jesus.

The world we live in says, "Go make something of yourself. You can do it. Find hope in your achievements."

The Gospel is different. It says any type of lasting hope is found only in Jesus. The Gospel proclaims our significance is found in Jesus. It is found in our union with him and being joined with him. Oh, how we struggle to find our significance in Jesus! Isaiah 2:22 says, *"Stop regarding man in whose nostrils is breath, for what account is he?"*

How much time do we worry about what others think of us? How much time do we spend worrying about how many likes our Instagram account has?

Our hearts crave the approval of others, but the Gospel breaks in and says, "Of what significance are others when I your God and king have given you everything and made you mine?"

The Gospel is good news of hope. The Gospel says that while we were still sinners, while we were looking for life and hope in anything and everything but God—this God demonstrated his love in that, while we were still sinners, Christ died for us (Rom. 5:8).

Christ entered into our brokenness and our idolatry. He came and lived the perfect life for you. He lived a life of righteousness where all his purpose and hope were found in the purposes of God. And he went to the cross where he took the punishment for all your sin, self-righteousness, and hopelessness.

Then on the third day, he rose again. He defeated death, sin, and hopelessness.

That is the hope of the Gospel. Is that your hope? Does this good news give you life and meaning and purpose? Does this good news fuel your hopes and dreams? Does this anchor your soul?

This good news changes everything.

When you see the glory of the Gospel and the love of God who has pursued you, even when you try to find life and hope in other things—it changes everything.

I love this picture in verse 2 that talks about the mountain of the house of the Lord being established as the highest of the mountains. Have you ever lived near a mountain range? I lived in Colorado Springs for a summer, and I love that city. I enjoyed exploring the fun things to do there, but I didn't have a clue how to get around. Luck-

ily, the conference center I worked at was near the base of Pikes Peak.
I could never get lost in Colorado Springs because all I had to do was
look up and see the towering mountain—"There's Pikes Peak. I know
the way home."

That is the good news of the Gospel. It is the only way home. In
John 14, Jesus has told the disciples he is going to the cross, and they
don't understand. Thomas says:

> Lord we do not know where you are going. How can we know the way?' Jesus
> said to him "I am the way, the truth and the life. No one comes to the Father
> except through me." (John 14:5–6)

Is Jesus your hope? Have you found hope in the Gospel? It is the
only hope we have. He's the way home for all of us.

The Mission of the Gospel

If this is your hope, it's one that cannot be contained. This hope
sends us out in mission.

Isaiah gives us an image of all the nations flowing to the mountain of God. The picture is of a river flowing, but instead of flowing
down, this river goes up. It is a great reversal. Instead of people
finding hope in themselves, they flow up and find hope in God.

Isaiah 2:3 says:

> Come, let us go up to the mountain of the LORD, to the house of the God of
> Jacob, that he may teach us his ways and that we may walk in his paths.

It's like the good news cannot be contained—"Come on, let's go to
the house of the Lord." Let's go to the place of hope.

It is not only a place of hope, but it is also a place of peace.

We were at enmity with God and with one another. God has made
peace with us. Jesus, the Prince of Peace, has not only made a way for
us to have a relationship with God, but we can also be reconciled
with one another. He is the true Prince of Peace, and he is coming
again. Then what we read about in Isaiah 2:4 will be a reality. It

doesn't mean we just look forward to that peace, but we are agents of it. We are on mission to bring this shalom in our world today.

This is the hope of the Gospel. Hope has broken into our world now—a hope for now and for what is not yet.

Hope fuels our mission. It is a big hope. Does hope fuel your life?

ISAIAH 6

I (Doug) am a huge St. Louis Cardinals fan. I grew up in Missouri and attended seminary in St. Louis. I moved there the summer of 1997 when Mark McGwire was hitting so many (steroid-helped) home runs, and the whole city went crazy over him. Everyone talked about whether he would break Roger Maris' record or not. My class-mates debated what date it might happen, and they bought tickets for the most likely times, trying to calculate which one game might be the difference-maker.

But my friend Brad and I took a different approach.

We each bought a ticket for *every* home game in September. We knew if he broke the record it would be late in the year, but we couldn't predict when. He might hit three in a game or go three games without a home run. That's the way the game worked.

So we bought two of the cheapest tickets we could get at $6 apiece, and we started going to a ton of games.

We were poor. I had just moved to St Louis and started seminary, so I took my New Testament Greek flashcards with me to review my homework. Brad and I left our families for baseball that fall. Thank you Julie and Dana for indulging us.

It was amazing!

I was there when McGwire hit home runs fifty and fifty-five and then sixty, sixty-one, and sixty-two. And I was there the last day of the season when he hit *both* sixty-nine and seventy.

It was glorious! When he hit number sixty-two, I thought I was being raptured. It seemed like the new heavens and new earth had come to us right then.

Flash forward a few years. Through some strange circumstances, I was able to meet and befriend J. D. Drew, who at the time also played for the Cardinals. In 2001, I went to Spring Training and stayed with J. D. in his condo in Florida, and I went to some games. I had access into the training room and clubhouse with him. He introduced me to Mike Matheny, Bobby Bonilla, and Tony LaRussa.

And just as we were leaving—Mark McGwire!

I nearly wet myself as I met my hero.

I said, "Hi Mark" and walked on.

So nonchalant. Like I meet home run king heroes every day. I didn't want to cause a scene, but I wanted to hang out with him.

In my mind, we were friends. I'd devoted a whole month to his cause, and I had planned on that month with many months of planning! And I knew J. D. Drew, and he knew Mark McGwire. Kevin Bacon's six degrees of separation wasn't even required. We were only two off.

I felt foolish. I didn't want to act like a fool, so I just wanted to play it cool and neither (cool nor fool) worked at all.

I felt small. He's a huge man. I'm not small, but compared to him I was a pipsqueak. I felt dumb, like I didn't know what to say at all. I was in the presence of greatness. And I did not come up looking very good.

That's the way it goes sometimes.

How do you feel when you come into the presence of greatness? Will you wilt like I did? It might be McGwire, Drummond, or DiMaggio. How would you react?

In chapter 2,, Isaiah saw God's enormous vision for the world—peace, prosperity, God's presence, and worship with the nations gathered.

But if we were to think of this sort of well-being, this shalom, (the Hebrew word for "peace") this goodness in our city—how in the world is this going to happen? Really. How?

Most of us would say, "Well, things are going to have to change." Who is the problem?

- Democrats
- Republicans
- Homeschoolers
- Private schoolers
- Public schoolers
- Pro-choicers
- Pro-lifers
- Greedy white-collar workers
- Deadbeat dads
- Freeloaders
- Walmart
- Communists
- Terrorists
- The illiterate
- The fundamentalists
- Politicians
- Texans
- Kids these days
- The SEC
- Boomers
- Millenials
- ??????

Somebody has to be the problem. If we could just fix *them*, then we'd be in business. That's how we're going to change the world.

Right?

In Isaiah 6, we're looking at what happens when a great person comes into the presence of a great God. This passage tells us why Isaiah writes this book in the first place, so it's like looking at an autobiography to find out more about what makes a man great. We're hoping to find some incentive to believe Isaiah 2 could actually happen.

We'll look at the three characters and then three actions.

Uzziah

Isaiah makes a point to root this incident in a specific time and place. He writes, *"In the year that King Uzziah died"* (6:1). You can find out about King Uzziah by looking back at 2 Chronicles 26, a part of the Bible that may not be bookmarked for you. Uzziah reigned for fifty-two prosperous and successful years, and he began his reign in godliness. He sought after God, and God blessed him.

However, here is a sentence in the Bible (or anywhere) you don't want to read about yourself: *"But when he was strong, he grew proud, to his destruction"* (2 Chron. 16:16). Uzziah tried to play God, and he boldly entered the temple, claiming for himself the rights God had only given the priests. The priests tried to stop him. But Uzziah raged in fury, and then leprosy broke out on his head. Uzziah was quarantined, and he died estranged, diseased, and alone.

This was a time of crisis for the nation. One commentator writes:

> Judah had known no king like Uzziah since the time of Solomon. He had been an efficient administrator and an able military leader. Under his leadership Judah had grown in every way (2 Chron. 26:1–15). He had been a true king. How easy it must have been to focus one's hopes and trust upon a king like that.[1]

The people must have been tempted to turn to whatever would work. They needed help. The king had died, so they're extremely vulnerable. They knew the nations around could swoop in and take over to fill the power vacuum. Assyria loomed in the background. It was a hostile nation known for carting its prisoners off with fish hooks in their mouths.

When we look around at world politics now, we see our time isn't that different. We wonder right now about Russia, North Korea, Syria, and the Middle East. Other countries aren't sure about us. What will we do in the climate we find ourselves in?

But if we get closer to home—what about for each of us?

What do you turn to in times of crisis?

What about when you get a new boss, department head, kindergarten teacher. little league manager, or a new yoga instructor?
We might be tempted to play God in our own homes and neighborhoods. We might try to establish our own vision for the way
things should go with our weddings, home projects, and parenting.
Where is your hope placed?

Do you ever ask, "Who is in charge here?"

Or do you assume you are, no matter what?

Isaiah

The next character in the story is marked by the word "I." Who is
that?

"I" is Isaiah Ben Amoz, the prophet who wrote this book. The
prophets often came from poverty and obscurity—but not Isaiah.

Jewish tradition tells us he came from nobility and was a recognized statesman, perhaps even a member of the royal family. Isaiah
had access to the courts of the day, and God used him to speak to the
kings.

Isaiah was a big shot, and he was in the power society. He had it
made.

And, as if that isn't enough, he was also considered the most holy
and righteous man of his day. So he was a good person at the highest
end of the social, political scene. He was definitely a Big Man On
Campus, BMOC. Big Man In Israel, BMII.

Is that you? Are you a good person? Are you from a good family, a
good job, a good major, a good career, a good sorority or fraternity, a
good morality structure? Are you a good friend or student or worker?

Most of us at least think we're better than *someone*. None of us
consider ourselves to be the bottom of the barrel. Most of us have
relatively high self-esteem. We come out the heroes of our stories.
We're over-comers of whatever hand is dealt to us.

When King Uzziah died in the midst of political confusion and
worry, Isaiah went to the temple to worship God. He was a good
man, high in social standing and religious morality. He didn't expect
what he found there. He met the third character in our narrative.

He met God.

God

Isaiah must have been shocked when this happened. Christians sometimes say, "I met God there" or "God's presence was really strong today."

That type of talking is all metaphor or second-hand meet and greet. It is not the same thing as, *"In the year that King Uzziah died I saw the Lord sitting upon a throne, high and lifted up; and the train of his robe filled the temple"* (Isa. 6:1).

You have to admit you would be surprised if this happened next Sunday. The last thing Isaiah expected to see when he went to church was—Yahweh!

What happens when Isaiah sees God?

The first surprise is that it happens at all. Isaiah saw him. The Jewish people believed that if anyone saw God he or she would instantly die. Various few individuals were allowed to see him, with an element of encouragement and confirmation involved.

The expectation for Isaiah, therefore, is he will soon be dead. (Which makes 1 John 3:2 all the more amazing: *"We know that when he appears we shall be like him, because we shall see him as he is."*)

What did Isaiah see when he saw God?

He saw the Lord. This isn't the personal name of God. That occurs in verse 5—you can tell when you see the all caps—LORD. This is "Lord." That is his title. He is the King. The Sovereign. The Lord. Kings sit on thrones, high and lifted up, with robes of majesty. This is the exalted king of the universe.

You might think we should learn more about what God looks like here. After all, wouldn't that be interesting and helpful knowledge? Commentator Oswalt writes:

> Words break down when one attempts to depict God himself.... There is a barrier beyond which the simply curious cannot penetrate. The experience is too personal, too awesome, too all-encompassing for mere reportage.[2]

All we know is there are seraphim around him. This is the only place we get this term about the seraphim, and we don't really know what these are except they're heavenly creatures, and the word "seraphim" means "fiery ones."

Awesome.

Terrifying.

It's one thing when you're at Spring Training, and you didn't expect to get to meet your favorite baseball player. Hello, Mark.

It's another thing when you meet God himself. Hello, Yahweh.

This is a big deal. He could show up any second. We pass this notion off because we don't believe it will happen. But we might want to reconsider that idea.

Annie Dillard writes:

> Why do people in churches seem like cheerful, brainless tourists on a packaged tour of the Absolute?... Does anyone have the foggiest idea what sort of power we so blithely invoke? Or as I suspect, does no one believe a word of it?... It is madness to wear ladies' straw hats and velvet hats to church; we should all be wearing crash helmets. Ushers should issue life preservers and signal flares; they should lash us to our pews. For the sleeping God may wake some day and take offense, or the waking God may draw us out to where we can never return[3]

What would it be like to go to church on Sunday and non-metaphorically meet God there?

Holiness

The seraphim propel us to our first action which isn't really an action at all. They are all wings and voice, perfectly ready for praise and service, typifying the appropriate response to God's holiness. Commentator Webb writes, "The seraphs, by their words and actions, show that the appropriate response is service and praise."[4] In Isaiah we read, *"And one called to another and said: "Holy, holy, holy is the Lord of hosts; the whole earth is full of his glory!"* (Isa. 6:3).

Here are these creatures flying around God, who sits on a throne in a king's and a judge's robe, and they are singing a specific song. They cry out, *"Holy, holy, holy."*

"Holiness" is a word you are familiar with if you hang out in church. But what does it mean? Holiness is transcendence—righteousness. Holiness is distinctiveness, uniqueness, otherness, and separateness. Holiness is superlative-ness.

If you put all these together, you can see that God alone deserves to be called holy in the true and ultimate sense of the word. But he does call other things holy. He sets things for holy uses. He separates them for distinctiveness. There is a moral quality to this, of righteousness and right use. When we talk about holy things or holy people we mean they are set apart for right use. But God always does the right thing, so his holiness is a quality he has in and of himself.

But the seraphim don't cry out, "Holy is the Lord of hosts!" They say, "Holy, holy, holy."

This is a peculiar aspect to Hebrew speech and writing. If you want to emphasize something, you repeat it.

We do that sometimes, but not in writing. In writing we underline or italicize or put an exclamation point. We wouldn't say, "That was a triple, triple, triple" to emphasize how Yadier Molina (a slow runner) hit a great triple. We'd say, "That was an [incredible/amazing/athletic/surprising] triple."

However, the Hebrew language repeats a word to emphasize it. A Hebrew author would say it's a triple, triple, triple [it's the triple of all triples].

In the New Testament, we see this when Jesus says, "Amen, Amen" which we translate "Truly, Truly." He's telling you he's about to say something important, which we believe to be the very words of God.

So you understand the device here. Very seldom do you ever get a word repeated three times for emphasis. And no other attribute of God is ever tripled. God is holy, holy, holy. Think about that. God isn't love, love, love or mercy, mercy, mercy or patient, patient, patient or just, just, just. He is holy, holy, holy.

One commentator writes, "His holiness is, therefore, his unapproachable and unique moral majesty before which sinful humankind instinctively quakes."[5] This holiness—righteous otherness—of God makes things shake and quake. You see smoke: *"And the foundations of the thresholds shook at the voice of him who called, and the house was filled with smoke"* (6:4).

I don't know what you think about this, but it is not boring.

Another aspect of holiness we don't often think about is that it really doesn't do anything for you.[6] God's holiness is completely non-functional for you. The only thing it might help you with is fear. God's love benefits you. So does his wisdom, strength, kingship, mercy, and justice.

But his holiness—how can you like that?

However, falling in love with God means you stop using him for what he gets you.[7] Let's say you are about to come into a big inheritance, and you fall in love and get engaged. Right before the wedding, you find out you won't be getting the money after all.

That's disappointing, but then your future spouse calls off the wedding. Why? Because he wanted you to get the money. You find out the money was a big part (or the main part) of his so-called love for you. How would you feel? Used, betrayed, and unloved.

That's how many of us treat God. We don't say it out loud, but we are thinking, "I will love you, God, if you give me stuff from your storehouse of blessings." But God says, "I want you to love me because of who I am. Because of my beauty, not my functionality."

That's what you want to hear in marriage, and God is much more beautiful and captivating than that. Can we love God for his holiness? Can we follow him for who he is, not for what we get out of it?

———

The seraphim also tell us one other thing.

They sing about God's holiness and glory unconfined to the temple. These attributes, and by extension God himself, fill the whole earth.

What do people do when they are in the presence of greatness?

I haven't been around greatness many times,[8] but it's always simultaneously attractive and disturbing. I went to a small enough high school that I was able to be involved in a ton of activities. I played baseball, football, and basketball. I played in the jazz band (jazz tuba!). I dabbled in some art and writing projects.

Not to brag on myself, but back in the day I started on my high school varsity basketball team. I was a decent player. I could have been much better. I used to dream of playing ball in college, but I learned that wasn't going to be a reality.

Since then, I've played basketball with Division I basketball players in various college rec centers. They are incredible. Absolutely incredible. When I was on the court with them, all of sudden I felt puny. Slow. I was made painfully aware of my lack of jumping ability. Of how I am not a good shooter.

So I'd shut off my game and start passing. These aren't even close to being the best basketball players in the world. There are better ones. What would it be like to play with Michael Jordan or LeBron?

Humbling. Embarrassing.

There are other situations like that. You're a good singer from a small town. Then you get to the university and find out you're the 1,000th best singer in your class.

Or you move to Nashville and find out there are 5,000 others better than you trying to make it.

You're a great painter from Ada, and you enter the art department and find out you can't pass your classes.

You're a charismatic person, and then you run into Barry Switzer, and you watch how he commands a room.

You're the homecoming queen, and then you join a sorority, and people think you're plain.

You're the math whiz, but you're struggling in the physics department.

You like to study the Bible and teach, and then you listen to Sinclair Ferguson for a day, and you're not quite as confident in your own abilities.[9]

We get in over our heads. We move from a big fish in a small pond to someone who's going to get eaten by the sharks. We may have overestimated our abilities and qualities.

What is it *you* think about yourself? You think you're pretty, fast, smart, a hard worker, righteous, moral, wise, a snappy dresser.... What is it?

You've walked into God at church. You're the only human in the room. However, there are other fiery creatures, and they are singing about God's incredible, magnificent, mind-blowing holiness. This should be both attractive and disturbing. You cannot believe what you're seeing, and you are instantly aware of your mediocrity and depravity.

In the presence of absolute holiness, every best part of me is rendered unclean, wrong, distorted, twisted. If your response isn't one of complete humility in the presence of such greatness, then you're missing something really important.

What do you do?

What do you feel?

Cleansing

Here's what you feel—terror.

You don't feel cozy or warm and fuzzy. You don't feel filled with the Spirit or special.

You feel terrified.

I've made a big deal out of overestimating ourselves. But there's a flip side, isn't there?

Some of us have been brought low over and over. We've been told we're good for nothing, and circumstances have borne this out. We've been called names, and we've been branded as losers. We've heard the prophetic voices of our parents, community, teachers, city leaders, and our pastors who have told us we are bad, bad people.

No good. Not worth it. Too far gone.

So we're not proud. We're ashamed and wracked with guilt.

We don't want to take up space or raise our voices because we've believed what others have said—we're doomed.

Isaiah speaks just like this. He's seen true goodness and holiness, and he's in big, big trouble. It's not like he's got a small blemish that needs to be cut off of in a minor out-patient surgery. He's been through the MRI, and every cell in his body has cancer. He's wrecked.

He writes:

> And I said: "Woe is me! For I am lost; for I am a man of unclean lips, and I dwell in the midst of a people of unclean lips; for my eyes have seen the King, the Lord of hosts!" (Isa. 6:5)

Commentator Webb writes:

> The vision of God produces not rapture but sheer terror in the
> prophet. He knows himself to be utterly ruined, for two reasons: he is
> unclean and he has seen God."[10]

I really don't like the ESV that translates the word "lost" there.
Lost? The word should be "undone," "ruined," "cut off," or
"destroyed." Other translations bring this out much better.

Not "lost," unless it means he has no hope at all. That sort of
utter lostness. This word "ruined/undone" is from "to be silenced."
To be silenced is to be dead. Those who have been buried have been
reduced to silence.

In other words—Isaiah is a goner.

Isaiah's first words are a pronouncement of woe on himself. He's
been declaring a lot of woe to others. Just back up and look at
chapter 5, which is a whole chapter filled with woe. Here's an
example starting in verse 20:

> Woe to those who call evil good and good evil, who put darkness for light and
> light for darkness, who put bitter for sweet and sweet for bitter! Woe to those
> who are wise in their own eyes, and shrewd in their own sight! Woe to those
> who are heroes at drinking wine, and valiant men in mixing strong drink, who
> acquit the guilty for a bribe, and deprive the innocent of his right! (Isa.
> 5:20–23)

Woe is bad. Real bad. You don't want to hear "woe."

But Isaiah isn't saying, "Woe are you!" He's not talking about the
bad people "out there." He's got the finger pointing to himself, and
now he's saying, "Woe is me!" This prominent, good person is
confirming judgment on himself.

In the presence of God, degrees of sin have become irrelevant. He
isn't comparing himself to anyone else. There's no sliding scale, no
grading on a curve, no allowances for the cost of living.

He's standing in the presence of the Holy God. And compared to
God, he's nothing.

This is the point where the prophet becomes aware of himself.

This is personal. He isn't talking about "them" anymore. He's talking about himself.

Before we go on, I want to talk about how we all have some guiding principle or outlook or worldview or Bible or functional deity. We've got to follow something.

Last week I was working out, and one of the women wore a t-shirt that said, "Do your own thing." Sounds awesome. However, she was following the instructions of the coach and the class, so I was unsure if her shirt was ironic or merely unfollowed t-shirt advice. If we all did our own thing, could we ever band together? How would we know if anything was good or bad?

Some of us follow Richard Dawkins as our prophet and guide. Some of us follow the Scientific Method. Some of us follow the faith and belief that "All truth is relative." Some of us have a baseline of what *Vogue* or *Seventeen* or *Popular Mechanics* or Apple or Fox News or *The Rolling Stone* or *The Atlantic* or ESPN Insider thinks.

Who is holy in our worlds? Who is at the top? Who has the authority to put us in our place?

God hasn't said one thing to Isaiah. Just being in God's presence makes Isaiah come apart. That's what "lost/undone" means. Isaiah is disintegrating. He's ruined. He's cut off. Eugene Peterson translates this as "doomsday" in *The Message*. Commentator Oswalt writes:

> Modern existential angst is a species of such despair, for confronted with the apparent meaninglessness of our existence in this universe, we wonder why we should go on living. Existentialism presumes no meaning in the universe and we are thus meaningless. Isaiah knows, more horribly, there is meaning, but he has no part in it.[11]

Isaiah writes, *"For I am a man of unclean lips, and I dwell in the midst of a people of unclean lips; for my eyes have seen the King, the Lord of hosts!"* (6:5). Isaiah's uncleanness is moral, and he's associating this with his heart not just his lips. What he talks about comes from his heart through his lips. He feels small in the presence of God, "but it is not the recognition of his finitude which crushes Isaiah; it is his uncleanness."[12] His character is in question.

Isaiah is ruined. He finds himself totally excluded from God and recognizes the consequence ("I am ruined") and the cause ("unclean lips"). Do you feel any sympathy for Isaiah here? Have you ever felt this way?

What do you think will happen next? Isaiah is willing to acknowledge his condition, but he expects to die right there on the spot. It's interesting Isaiah doesn't cry out for mercy or vow to do better. He has put his head on the block, knowing he deserves whatever he gets. What he gets, then, is all from God's initiative.

He doesn't die. God rescues him.

One of the seraphim goes to the altar, takes a burning coal, and comes at Isaiah's mouth with it. He touches Isaiah's felt need—his lips—but cleanses Isaiah's real cause—the guilt, inner corruption, and real wrong he has done. The seraphim say, *"Behold, this has touched your lips; your guilt is taken away, and your sin atoned for"* (6:7).

"Your guilt is taken away, and your sin atoned for." Those are beautiful, life-giving words. Commentator Webb writes:

> The coal and altar symbolize the entire provision which God had made in the temple and its services for the sins of his people. Isaiah is cleansed, not by his own efforts, but purely by the grace of God.[13]

Motyer adds:

> The live coal thus encapsulates the ideas of atonement, propitiation, satisfaction, forgiveness, cleansing, and reconciliation, and of these spiritual realities to Isaiah, the erstwhile doomed sinner, is left in no doubt when the seraph explains: "Behold, as soon as this touched your lips your iniquity went, and, as for your sin—paid by ransom!"[14]

This sounds like 1 John 1:8–9:

> *If we say we have no sin, we deceive ourselves, and the truth is not in us. If we confess our sins, he is faithful and just to forgive us our sins and to cleanse us from all unrighteousness.*

Jesus forgives us of our sins. He paid the debt. He paid the price with his life. He took the penalty so we could experience true fellowship, oneness, and intimacy with God. He gave us his righteousness and holiness, so we could be one with God.

So you've done things wrong. I hope we're all able to admit that. Many of us have been accused of things we haven't done. So be it.

When we traveled to Columbia, Missouri, for my daughter Ruth's graduation, I left explicit instructions to make sure *all* the dishes were put in the dishwasher and the counters were left clean. I didn't want Julie to have to return to a messy kitchen, and we were gone over Mother's Day.

When we returned from our trip on Monday, we found a kitchen that had not been taken care of. Who did it? Who was guilty?

I have my theories, but the thing was—I wanted a clean kitchen for my wife, my best friend. I hadn't dirtied those dishes, but I cleaned them anyway. The responsibility ended up being mine. I paid the price. It was a small price to pay, but I still paid it.

I'm saying you may have created unclean dishes, but they still have to be washed. Who will clean them? You?

What if you left a ton of dirty dishes, and yet on Monday afternoon they were cleaned and put away? What if all were forgiven and all was set right? What if dignity were restored and shame was taken away? What if there were grace in this world, even for you?

And surely it's true we haven't been caught for every wrong thing we've done, have we? While we may be falsely accused, there have been times when we've gotten away with things.

Some are tiny. I snuck money out of my mom's purse when I was a kid. I've not obeyed the speed limit a thousand times more than what I've gotten tickets for. I've cheated on my diet and not logged all my calories. I've hated in my heart. I've cursed under my breath (and out loud to parishioners). I've acted patient, but not been patient. I've left things undone.

So perhaps I've got a bit of a skewed perspective on how mistreated I've been. Maybe I've been afforded far more general grace than I realize. Perhaps if I'm under the bright light of God's holiness, I might see those blemishes and imperfections far more clearly.

But we're not talking about that!

We're talking about seeing ourselves for who we really are— sinners saved by grace! All of us! Everyone.

Whether you're a dignified, wealthy prophet in the Ancient Near East or a single parent from the suburbs—you are loved by God because of the grace of Jesus. Whether you're eight or eighty. Whether you're from the city, the country, or the backwoods. Whether you're notorious or you fly under the radar. Whether you're a goody two-shoes or a committed rebel.

Sin is real. It's bad.

But forgiveness is real too. It's great. God isn't only holy, holy, holy. He is that. He's also gracious, kind, forbearing, and compassionate to thousands of generations. He fulfills his own covenants. He sent his only son Jesus to live under the law, and yet to die under God's wrath, to bear the weight and penalty of sins he did not commit, and to be buried, and then to rise again on the third day.

Your record can be wiped completely clean. Your dignity is restored. You are set free in Christ.

That's the good news! He's come for you in love.

Commissioning

Forgiveness is real, and it's powerful. Grace is something God gives us in Christ. Anne Lamott writes:

> It is unearned love—the love that goes before, that greets us on the way. It's the help you receive when you have no bright ideas left, when you are empty and desperate and have discovered that your best thinking and most charming charm have failed you. Grace is the light or electricity or juice or breeze that takes you from that isolated place and puts you with others who are as startled and embarrassed and eventually grateful as you are to be there.[15]

If you have experienced this grace, then you'll have a response. Look at what happens next in 6:8: *"And I heard the voice of the Lord saying, 'Whom shall I send, and who will go for us?' Then I said, 'Here am I! Send me.'"*

God speaks for the first time. After Isaiah has been given the grace of forgiveness, God issues him a call.

Isaiah discovers being joined to God also means joining a

missionary society. Oswalt comments: "God makes it plain that while spiritual experience is never merely a means to an end, neither is it an end in itself."[16] Isaiah discovers he has been brought in—in order to be sent out.[17] The Lord seeks a messenger, and Isaiah, now cleansed, is ready and willing to be his mouthpiece.[18] Now, as a redeemed sinner, Isaiah is free to speak. Here is Oswalt again:

> Having believed with certainty that he was about to be crushed into non existence by the very holiness of God and having received an unsought for, unmerited, complete cleansing, what else would he rather do than hurl himself into God's service? Those who need to be coerced are perhaps too little aware of the immensity of God's grace toward them.[19]

God did not annihilate Isaiah's personal identity. Isaiah says, *"Here am I."* He still had an "I," an identity, a personality.

God didn't destroy the self but redeemed it. It was overhauled but not gone. Isaiah made an offering of himself, just like we read in Romans 12:1–2:

> *I appeal to you therefore, brothers, by the mercies of God, to present your bodies as a living sacrifice, holy and acceptable to God, which is your spiritual worship. Do not be conformed to this world, but be transformed by the renewal of your mind, that by testing you may discern what is the will of God, what is good and acceptable and perfect.*

Can you say, "Here am I" to God? He's a really big God. He created a really big universe and has a massive plan of redemption. Can God be more real to you than your needs? Can you be available to God, no matter what? Isaiah offers himself to God even before God tells him the job description.

That is availability for sure. Isaiah's job wasn't a great one. He was supposed to preach to people who would never come around. That's what the rest of Isaiah 6 tells us. Boo! Personal fulfillment wasn't on the top of Isaiah's agenda. Following the Holy God of grace was what God wanted for Isaiah.

Could you volunteer more of your time? Could you sacrifice your time? As you get to be older and understand grace more deeply, could you be more gripped by the needs of people in this world, instead of less so? Could you give more money than you think, even sacrificially, instead of none at all, or just enough so it doesn't really affect you? Could your generosity actually change the way you live? Could you volunteer for a job at the church that doesn't get you any applause or thank yous?[20]

When you have God as a reality like this, you also have to have a hope. It might look like that won't happen, but it will. The last verse in Isaiah 6 tells us so. There is a seed in the stump (we'll talk about this soon). As Tolkien wrote, Everything sad will come untrue. Things are going to change. You may not see it, but it is happening. Do you believe in this? Does this grip you? Wouldn't this affect the world? Would it change your church? Your city?

One of the things I like to point out in narratives or stories is you should make an attempt to associate yourself with someone in the story. But, remember this, you're never God or Jesus. You're almost always the worst person in the story. That's who you should identify with.

Who are you in this story?

Uzziah? He lived a good life, but he died in seclusion and shame because of his pride. I don't know if we'll see him in heaven or not. The text doesn't indicate the definitive answer, though I think it shades us toward a positive outcome. Are you Uzziah? Do you think you can use God? Do you think you can use church and its sacraments according to your own wishes?

Or are you Isaiah? Isaiah had a personal experience based on a transcended truth. He nearly died when he met God. He thought he was going to. He saw the holy, holy, holy God and almost came apart. He would have but for God's grace and atonement for him.

Has that ever happened to you? Do you believe in a conceptual, friendly God? Do you think he's all and only cuddly love? Do you ever quake before him?

If you're not Isaiah, then do you have an experience with this God? Jeremiah's experience was different from Isaiah's, but he had one. Paul's was different, but he met God on the road. There is no "one way" this happens, but it has to happen. We need to meet God.

If you really know God, you'll shake and quake sometimes. He won't conform to your conceptions. He'll baffle you. He'll mystify you. He'll reorder your priorities. He won't change your agenda. He'll give you a whole new agenda.[21] He'll send you out with a mission.

Has that happened? Do you recognize yourself as a sinner? As lost? As needy? I'm not talking about low self-esteem, which is usually self-absorption, but I'm asking if you have seen yourself as nothing when stacked up against real glory, holiness, and superlativeness. I'm talking about reality. And if you don't see yourself this way, then you just haven't seen God.

Have you really seen *God*? Do you know of a time when God switched from being a concept to a reality?

Perhaps you have yet to see God's forgiveness and his atonement for you. He needs to touch your lips and your heart. Once he does, then you have a mission. You have a new agenda. You have a message. You have a commissioning, a calling.

One second after you realize you are more wicked and flawed than you ever dared believe, you also realize you are more loved and cherished through the grace of God than you ever could have ever thought possible.[22] It wasn't performance. It wasn't standards. It was grace. That is amazing. It is a bold humility. A new stability. That can change the world.

Jesuit priest and LA inner city missionary Gregory Boyle tells stories in his book *Tattoos on the Heart*. He ministers among gang members, gangbangers, prostitutes, and the poor. He tells stories about how he saw himself in the lives of the people he's around every day, but he needed to be around people who lived the way they did. He writes they "had some privileged delivery system for giving me access to the Gospel. Naturally, I wanted to be around this."[23]

In one story, Cesar gets out of jail and he calls up Gregory to see if he can help him get some clothes. He doesn't have any. Gregory helps him out. They're in JC Penny, and Cesar looks scary. He talks rough.

But Cesar doesn't want to go back to jail. He's the one who's scared.

Gregory writes that years before, he had had a change of strategy in ministering to those around him. Instead of busting in on people or reforming them, he started trying to catch them doing the right thing and affirm it. Instead of being harsh and exacting, he'd talk about how heroic and courageous they were to attempt to transform their lives, how they were giants among men. He'd throw them off balance that way.

So when Cesar says he's scared to go back to jail, Gregory responds this way: "Look son, who's got a better heart than you? And God is at the center of that great, big ol' heart. Hang on to that dog—cuz you have what the world wants. So what can go wrong?"[24]

They say goodbye, but then Gregory gets a phone call that wakes him up at 3 a.m. It's Cesar, and he says it's urgent they talk.

Cesar says, "I gotta ask you a question. You know how I've always seen you as my father—ever since I was a little kid? Well, I hafta ask you a question." He pauses underneath the gravity of it all.

Boyle writes that Cesar asks in a wavering voice,

"Have I... been... your son?"

"Oh, hell, yeah," I say.

Now his voice becomes enmeshed in a cadence of gentle sobbing. "Then... I will be... your son. And you... will be my father. And nothing will separate us, right?"

"That's right."

In this early morning call Cesar did not discover he was a father. He discovered he was a son worth having. The voice broke through the clouds of his terror and the crippling mess of his own history, and he felt himself beloved. God, wonderfully pleased in him, is where God wanted Cesar to reside.[25]

———

Jesus was undone for you. He was broken. No seraphim came to help him when God turned from him. The temple shook when Jesus died on the cross. Because he was undone, you can be made right. Because he took the fire, you can be healed with it.

It means God loves you. Tattoo that on your heart. You're a beloved son, a beloved daughter. Grace matters. Be free in Christ.

ISAIAH 7, 9, 11

Although greatness is inspiring, it can also be disturbing, and it unsettles us.

But there is another scenario—when you are around greatness before you even realize it.

One of my (Doug's) friends grew up with a buddy down in Mississippi in the 70s and 80s. He was on the football squad, and they had a pretty good team. They'd all hang out and go over to a friend's house and watch movies until 2 a.m.

They dominated on the field. They ran the ball pretty much every play, and that's how they won. But every once and awhile, the quarterback would have to scramble, and then he'd let loose a pass that would go seventy yards in the air, and everyone would be in shock.

That quarterback got one—one!—Division I scholarship offer, and he took it to play football at the University of Southern Mississippi. That quarterback, my friend's buddy who was just a nobody back then, was and is Brett Favre, one of the best to ever play the game. But back then, he was just Brett, an idiot high school kid from a no-name town in Mississippi.

Have you ever been around greatness and didn't realize it? Have you ever figured it out way after the fact? Or have you ever seen the seeds of greatness in someone, and then watched it grow over time?

It can take time to recognize greatness before it is evident to everyone. These three passages in Isaiah 7, 9, and 11 are like that. They show us what we should be looking for in greatness. They point to it almost a thousand years before it came, and they still point to it today. Let's see if chapters written 2,700 years ago might have any relevance to us today. Let these ancient texts speak to our hearts and enlarge our vision.

Isaiah 7—A Child Born of a Virgin

The context of Isaiah 7 is what we've been discussing thus far. King Ahaz has taken over from King Uzziah who has died (chapter 6). Ahaz was afraid of all the nations around him, so he began making treaties. Judah has been routed, and now the armies were coming for Jerusalem.

Ahaz was shaking in his boots, so he turned to Assyria which would prove to be a tragic choice. He sold out his people in order to keep his job. Perhaps he thought he was doing the right thing, but he subjugated the people, and he dishonored God.

Ahaz has become a puppet king for Tiglath-Pileser. If you flip/scroll over to 2 Kings 16, you'll read how Ahaz sacrificed his own son, which is a rite for the Assyrian god Molech. He made an altar in Damascus to worship the Assyrian gods. He called himself the Assyrian king's servant and his son. This is some bad mojo going on. He's demoted Yahweh into a minor deity because he's afraid of the Syrians and Egyptians. He's looking at pragmatic politics, which is perhaps what good leaders do. But not godly leaders. Not God's kings.

Ahaz does whatever it takes to save himself, and he thinks he's saving his nation. Except he doesn't trust God. Isaiah tells Ahaz, "You won't be completely wiped out. These nations won't last. They'll be defeated. Trust me. Follow God. Have faith. Ahaz, stand firm!" That's what he means when he says, *"If you are not firm in the faith, you will not be firm at all"* (Isa. 7:9).

What would you do if a prophet told you this in your time of crisis? Would you follow his advice?

Isaiah tells Ahaz to ask for a sign to reassure him. In 7:11, we read, *"Ask a sign of the LORD your God; let it be deep as Sheol or high as heaven."*

Don't you think Ahaz should ask for a sign since God told him to do so? But Ahaz was dripping with pious, super spiritual, church talk. He said, *"'I will not ask, and I will not put the LORD to the test'"* (7:12).

When God tells you to look for a sign, you should ask for one! Ahaz said he didn't want to make demands on God. He'd go his own way. He wants to stay in control, so he won't ask.

God got mad, and through Isaiah, he told Ahaz, "You're going to get a sign anyway." Isaiah wrote, *"Therefore the Lord himself will give you a sign. Behold, the virgin shall conceive and bear a son, and shall call his name Immanuel"* (Isa. 7:14).

In the midst of crisis, fear, and judgment, you will get a miraculous conception. This child will come into a desolate god-forsaken place.

Ahaz chose not to trust God.

We have the Ahaz Question—will you look for the signs God gives you?

Other questions spring off of this one. Is your mind already made up as to how God will save? Have you already decided how the world works, or can God intervene with you? What are you basing your assurance on? What is your belief resting upon? What evidence are you waiting for before you will have faith?

And if you do trust God and ask him for a sign, what if he gives you a really strange one? Like: *"Therefore the Lord himself will give you a sign. Behold, the virgin shall conceive and bear a son, and shall call his name Immanuel"* (Isa. 7:14).

In the midst of judgment, God will send a baby boy named God With Us through the body of a virgin girl.

Don't be fooled. Not all is well. There is judgment, as we read in the rest of the passage after this virgin birth announcement. The text says God will whistle at flies and bees, two insects not known for taking commands. These are judgments reminiscent of the plagues in Egypt. They'll infest every nook and cranny.[1]

When God says he'll take the razor, it means he's going to emasculate those who need to be judged. He'll leave them "shamed, exposed, and denuded."[2] People will consider themselves lucky to have anything at all. Vineyards will become weed patches and thorn bushes.

When God sets things right, he sets evil to wrong. He judges what needs correcting.

And he will send a baby to a virgin.

Now, I don't want to conduct a sex-ed class, but... virgins don't give birth. However, I did a bit of research and found a longitudinal study that tracked nearly 8000 girls as they entered puberty in 1995 and then for fourteen years into adulthood in 2008. These women were asked to consider their pregnancies.[3] Forty-five of these 8000 females claimed a virgin birth for their pregnancies.

If you were to trace back the reasons for these virginal claims, you'd find that these young women signed chastity pledges and had poor communication with parents. Though it's tough for the researchers to test data under these self-reporting circumstances, women still claim virgin births. (Do not try this virgin birth excuse at home with your self-righteous parents. They may not believe you.)

The word translated "virgin" can also mean "young woman." There is a specific word for virgin that could have been used. This is the ambiguous term *alma* instead of the unambiguous *betula*. *Alma* means "a young woman of marriageable age," but the term is never used of married women in the Old Testament. So the word denotes a sexually mature but unmarried young woman, which is commonly understood in the Hebrew society to mean a virgin. "Maiden" gets at it well.

The ambiguous nature of a sign is part and parcel with prophecies, isn't it?

Maher Shalal Hash Baz (whose name means "the spoil speeds, the prey hastens") is the next child mentioned in the Bible after this prophecy. But Maher Shalal Hash Baz—was he born of a virgin? Is he Immanuel, God with us? No. He had a father. He's not Immanuel.

We need to keep looking. There are miraculous birth stories all over the place.[4] Both the Assyrians and the Babylonians had them. Buddha's unusual birth story developed over the centuries. There are Greco, Roman, and Chinese birth narratives that seem strange. The Aztecs have them.

For centuries, the prophecy had floated around, but no one knew exactly what it meant. A boy will be born from a virgin in an obscure land. This child will have strong and special powers. He would grow strong and defeat evil, restore good and set things right again. But who was he?

Anakin Skywalker?[5]

Could any of these be true? What if one might be?

We're looking at these three Isaiah texts together to see if they have anything to say to us. It's more important than considering virginity or prophecies that don't come true.

This passage is really a Christmas message. If you're reading this, but it's not in December, it's perfect for you to hear about the meaning of Christmas. You don't have to buy any presents or go to any parties. No tacky sweaters. You don't have to hear about baby Jesus in a manger. No "Santa Baby."

Do you understand Christmas? Is Christmas about love, goodness, giving, and making the world a better place? We hear Christmas is like the 1985 "We are the World" song: "We are the world, we are the people. We are the ones who make a better day, so let's start giving."

Has the hope of Christmas faded from your memory? Have you moved on to visions of summer trips, projects, and whatever else consumes your time and energy?

Does a miracle seem too impossible for you?

A baby boy will be born to a virgin, and his name shall be called Immanuel, God with us. God will come miraculously close.

Isaiah 9—Will Be the Ideal Forever Ruler

As I've read about and studied King Henry VIII, I'm not sure I can come up with a more conflicted, confusing, and somewhat-creative king. I'm tempted to say there has been none worse, but that's probably not true. There have been worse.

Henry's problem was he was so human, and he had so much power to carry out his every desire. That would destroy any of us. He managed to set England in a fairly good position because of his advisors around him, but he used every possible strategy at his disposal to accomplish his own whims.

I'm sure by the end of Henry's life, whenever a statement went out from the King's chambers, everyone rolled their eyes. He was truly, literally unbelievable.

Sounds a little like "I am not a crook," " orI did not have sexual relations with that woman," or "There are weapons of mass destruction in Iraq," or "The election was stolen." Or what happens every day in our news.

We Americans don't like kings. It's in our DNA to rally against them. Power corrupts, and absolute power corrupts absolutely. No taxation without representation. The Boston Tea Party. George Washington deciding not to run for president again.

But... what if? What if the king were right, good, true, pure, honorable, and virtuous? Wouldn't that be a good situation? Couldn't we prosper and thrive under good and godly leadership?

Chapter 9 of Isaiah begins with the word "But." The NIV translation says, "Nevertheless." If you read chapter 8 (and remember the woes in chapter 5) along with much of the first part of the book to this point, you'll see the world is a bad place.

But you knew that, didn't you? Girls are put into prostitution at nine years old. They are abused all over the world. People are taken advantage of financially and economically. People are caught in situations they cannot get out of. Ethnic cleansing is a reality in our world still today. We have nuclear weapons ready to fire. Countries are incredibly unstable, and long-time rulers seem to topple and then rise again every month. Our budget is in shambles. Our school system is bankrupt. There are looming pandemics.

Nevertheless... *"there will be no gloom for her who was in anguish"* (9:1).

Do you believe in a "nevertheless"?

Do you have some sort of hope? What is that hope placed in today? Where does that hope rest? That we can make a better world, just you and me? That was sung years ago, and has it happened?

After the Ahaz Question (Will you look for the signs God gives you?), the Nevertheless-Moment here tells us our way leads to darkness, but God's way leads to light. This oracle of salvation rejects the way of Ahaz, the way of the world. It points us to something different, something more. It points to a coming king who will set all things right.

Christianity is extremely realistic. It doesn't say the world is a great place, and you just have to see it that way. It doesn't say if we'd only all get together, goodness would come out of us, and we'll have restoration. Christianity says that this world is broken and sinful. We need a ruler to love, redeem, guide, and show us the way.

Isaiah 9 tells us there will be a king, but he's not what you'll expect. Commentator Webb writes:

> The outworking of God's purpose in history through the whole of chapters 7–9 is associated with (either figuratively or literally) the birth of children. Truly his strength is made perfect in weakness.[6]

So we're going to have a child king. That never seems to go well.

The prophecy keeps getting more far-fetched. In Isaiah 9:1, we read that this king will come from Galilee. This is like saying someone will come from the panhandle of Oklahoma. People don't come from there, well no one of much importance or notoriety. I've driven through the panhandle, and here's not much to see.

Things happen in the big city. But this child will be from the backwaters, the least likely place.

And, and this is really weird, this child from the region of Galilee will be God himself. The language can only apply to one who is God incarnate. God-With-Us. Immanuel. The expected, perfect king will be both human and divine.

The language makes another point. It underlines the central paradox in Isaiah's conception of Yahweh's deliverance of his people. How will God deliver his people from arrogance, war, oppression, and coercion? By being more arrogant, more warlike, more oppressive, and more coercive?

Will God fight power with power? The book of Isaiah frequently proclaims God is powerful enough to destroy his enemies in an instant. Yet, again and again, when the prophet comes to the heart of the means of deliverance, a childlike face peers out at us. God is strong enough to overcome his enemies by becoming vulnerable, transparent, and humble—the only hope, in fact, for turning enmity into friendship.

It was common in the Ancient Near East to have fantastic titles of kingship, such as Mighty Bull Appearing in Thebes and Enduring in Kingship like Re in Heaven. We might be familiar with "All hail His Grace, Joffrey of Houses Baratheon and Lannister, First of His Name, King of the Andals and the First Men, Lord of the Seven Kingdoms, and Protector of the Realm."[7]

What we have here in Isaiah 9 is not a coronation hymn but a joyful birth announcement. We see those all the time now, don't we? When women are pregnant, everyone has to know about it. Get ready, there's a baby on board. And now it's time for the gender reveal!

Somehow, and the text hasn't told us how yet, a virgin-born child will demonstrate that God is with us. We know it will be a miracle, and this child will have traits manifesting the presence of God in our midst. This Virgin Birth Miracle Son will unleash a great celebration! Way bigger than a video on Facebook.

When God created the world, he separated light from darkness, and he created the sun and stars. God creates out of the dark, expansive nothingness of nothing, and he can still do it. He can shine light into any dark situation, and we all know a little light can go a long way. But this light won't be sparing. It will be sunbursts.

Joy abounds in Isaiah 9 as God promises deliverance of his people under the rule of this new miraculous king. There will be festivals, multiplication, gifts, and greetings. God will justly judge the wicked.

We finally get to the heart of the matter, the naming of the attributes in this joyful announcement, and then we sing!

Queue up the music from Handel's Messiah:

"And the government will be upon his shoulders....

And his name shall be call-ed..."

Wonderful Counselor[8]—or "wonder of a counselor." The word "wonder" suggests something supernatural and beyond human comprehension. The folly of human wisdom is derided because the coming one will give wondrous counsel, unfailing in the depth of its wisdom.

True wisdom knows that in wisdom is strength, in surrender is victory, and in death is life (John 12:24–26). This counselor will be truly amazing.

I think everyone needs counseling. I tell my church that all the time. Some counselors are lousy. They don't listen well, or they hand out too much advice. Some take the easy way out.

But you'll know it when you're in the midst of a truly wonderful counselor. Julie and I had one named Bruce. We drove three hours to Dallas for a two-hour session, and then we headed back home. We signed up for a monthly, eight-hour day because we needed the help in our marriage.

Jesus is our Wonderful Counselor. He's better than Bruce.

Mighty God—Great hero. This term always refers to God (Deut. 10:17, Jer. 32:18). This is a title for Yahweh. It's not really "a mighty God" but more "the one and only mighty God." When I was a kid, the youth football league was called Mighty Mites, which is a clever name.

God's no mighty mite. He's the Mighty God. Almighty is his name.

The king will have God's true might about him, a power so great it can absorb all the evil which can be hurled at it until none is left to hurl. He's big and strong, mighty to save.

Everlasting Father—Forever fatherhood, and that's a mighty long time. He'll leave a legacy that endures forever.

Is this just Ancient Near Eastern bombast? No, this is never found in Israel's writing for its human kings. God's fatherhood doesn't impose itself upon his children but sacrifices for them. (Rom. 8:15–17, Luke 23:34) We've been let down by fathers but not this one. He'll always be there.

. . .

Prince of Peace—someone who comes in peace and establishes peace, not by a brutal squashing of all defiance but by means of a transparent vulnerability which makes defiance pointless.

I love Prince. I grieved his death. Any time I hear "Purple Rain," I stand up and sing in tribute. But Prince is dead, may he rest in peace.

However, the Prince of Peace still lives! Through him will comes the reconciliation between God and man that makes possible reconciliation between man and God. (Luke 2:14, John 16:33, Rom. 5:1, Hebr. 12:14). He's the prince of shalom, of wholeness and flourishing.

This new king will rule in fairness and justice. He'll treat people well. He won't sell out like Ahaz or any other ruler. He's not making deals. He's making all things new.

There was one who came 700 years later who was called Son of God, First Among Men, Leader, and Glorious. Do you know who that was?

Caesar Augustus. He was considered a god, and he brought the *Pax Romana* (the peace of Rome) to the world. Was he who we were looking for?

He was a great hero for sure (for some).

But he's not the hero Isaiah's thinking of. He's not even close. He didn't fulfill the prophecy.

Do you need a counselor? Do you need a hero? Do you need a father? Do you need peace? Do you need a light? Isaiah 9:2 says, *"The people who walked in darkness have seen a great light; those who dwelt in a land of deep darkness, on them has light shined."* So yes, we all need counselors, heroes, fathers, peace, and light.

You need light shined into the dark places of your heart and life. So do I. Where can we get these things?

Isaiah 9:3 says there will be an increase in joy. How could light, joy, a wonderful counselor, a mighty God, an everlasting father, and a prince of peace ever occur in one person, however great he might be?

Even if he (or she) had all these things, this person can't live forever, and then we're stuck all over again. This is one of the recurring themes of Jewish and in all of history. Just when you get a great leader with all power and wisdom focused together, he or she dies, and then the person next in line screws it all up. Uzziah did great but ended poorly. After him, we have Ahaz. Nothing good ever seems to last. There's a term limit for everyone in the end.

What hope is there?

A child born of a virgin will be the ideal ruler....

Let's look at our last text, Isaiah 11, to see if it helps.

Isaiah 11—Who Will Be the Root of Jesse

Isaiah 11 reads like a Serven home maintenance project. I chainsawed a ton of scrub trees at our house in Norman,[9] but I always left the stumps in the ground. I considered a stump grinder, but they are expensive and complicated, and I learned to consider my track record for home improvement projects (I'm terrible at them).

Every spring, I had to clip off the little saplings that grew out of the stumps.

I don't like stumps.

Isaiah 11 tells me I'm right to hate these stumps. When the tree has been cut down, the stump is left as a reminder of what used to be there. The dynasty of David is in disarray, in disaster, deforested. What used to be glorious is now cut down and rendered as nothing, a stump ready to be ground up.

Christianity brings us another honest picture. David was a great king—and a great screw up, especially at the end of his life with his dealings with women and children. He left a very mixed legacy of brokenness in his family. And now here we are with Ahaz seemingly sealing the fate of the people of God by consigning them to Assyrian slavery.

We live in darkness, and we are surrounded by it—physical, sexual, and emotional abuse. Depression. Debt. Prison. Being forgotten or overlooked or passed over. A lack of fairness or justice. Death. Cancer. Miscarriages. These are stumps lying all throughout the rainforest—reminders that this world is not what it is supposed to be.

It makes me think of what C. S. Lewis writes about Narnia in the beginning of *The Lion, the Witch and the Wardrobe*: "It's always winter and never Christmas." That's what our lives often feel like. Cold, dark, and hopeless.

It's like it's always February. Snow days are fun at first. But after a few of them stack up, we get bored, and the snow turns grey and mushy. February is a tough month. Christmas is over, and spring is still a ways away. It's cold and dark most of the day. February is the Tuesday of months. Not even close to the weekend.

Are you feeling February today? "Stumpy" isn't the best nickname you could have, but it's where many of us live life, and it's how Isaiah describes God's people. It doesn't matter they did it to themselves. They're looking at their land of stumps in a place that used to be majestic forests.

Just like Israel, you need the hope of a shoot from the stump. Isaiah says there will be another David someday soon, another ruler who will set everything right.... Right...?

Oh, I wish it could be true.

But you know what happens to shoots—I come along and clip them off or spray them so they never come back. They don't make it. You want another messiah? Another king? Do you really think a different king will save you? You'll just say to me, "I've tried those, and they don't work." And, do you know what? You're right to be cynical.

And yet, think about this—in our stump-like lives, why is it so difficult to utterly and completely extinguish hope? Why do we hope for a shoot at all? Isn't it more real and honest to behave like the existentialists and nihilists and give up all hope? Can't we get real and understand this is all there is and all there will ever be? Dog eat dog. Survival of the fittest. The slow grinding toward getting extinguished.

I don't think we can sustain such complete angst. You can't turn off your hope because of the way you've been designed by God. You were built for more than this. It's just you don't know what *this* is yet.

Maybe your hope is not wrong after all. Read Isaiah 11. There might be a king who rules with the Spirit of the Lord, with wisdom and understanding, with counsel and might, with knowledge and the fear of the Lord. He'll be a good and gracious judge who loves and serves the poor and the meek, and who goes against evil in his goodness. Those who are weak will have a place with those who are strong. Those who would use each other will instead serve each other. Perhaps there is a time and place, if not today then someday, where we don't use and devour each other, but we walk together in all our created, natural differences. What a day that might be, the day of the Lord, a day where a full knowledge of the Lord cannot be contained even by the oceans.

It's not another shoot you need. Shoots come and go. They are anything temporary you can put your hope in. But there is something else. 11:10 tells us it will be a *shoot* from the *root*.

It's not just another messiah or king, president, governor, headmaster, city council woman, or FBI Director. We're looking for something more! It's not just another way for us to repair ourselves so we can have personal peace and affluence. No, instead, as we read on in chapter 11, the whole world will be radically healed by this kingdom. Everything made right. The root of Jesse makes this happen (Isa. 11:10). Not the offspring or stump of Jesse, but the author of Jesse.

Who or what is the root of Jesse? This has to be God himself. He is the author of Jesse, David, and you. There is no reason to hope in the shoot if it's just another shoot. But if the shoot is the root, then we have something. If God breaks through and walks among us, then we have a reason to hope.

———

Okay, so that's great. According to Isaiah, we're looking for a child born of a virgin who will be the ideal forever ruler and the root of Jesse.

Let's look again at the Christmas story for our Advent message. We need to look to Jesus.

Working backward from our outline, we see Jesus was not only from the line of Jesse but was in fact the root of Jesse. Matthew 1 gives Jesus' genealogy, tracing it back to David and Jesse. He is from the right line.

What is more, John 1 tells us Jesus is the Word of God. He was with God from the very beginning. He made everything, and nothing was made without him. That is the ultimate root of Jesse, and of everything. I cannot prove this to you. You have to believe it or not.

Do you believe Jesus is God? Do you think he is the Word made flesh, the second person of the Trinity, fully man and fully God? That is a huge idea, one with enormous implications in your life if it might be true.

It should fill you with all sorts of ideas and joy—or dread. It should affect you in many ways. It should mean you have a rootedness no one can take away from you.

Do you believe it?

Is Jesus the ideal ruler?

The Westminster Larger Catechism states Jesus fulfilled the offices of prophet, priest, and king. To answer how, it asks and then answers this question:

> Q. 45. How doth Christ execute the office of a king?
> A. Christ executes the office of a king, in calling out of the world a people to himself, and giving them officers, laws, and censures, by which he visibly governs them; in bestowing saving grace upon his elect, rewarding their obedience, and correcting them for their sins, preserving and supporting them under all their temptations and sufferings, restraining and overcoming all their enemies, and powerfully ordering all things for his own glory, and their good; and also in taking vengeance on the rest, who know not God, and obey not the gospel.

There are a ton of Bible references that would help you look at this concept of Jesus's ministry as prophet, priest, and king. Working through those texts would surely be helpful, but if you look through the Gospels, you will discover the writers took great pains to show Jesus was indeed a king, however an unorthodox and surprising one. He was not what the people either expected or wanted, but he was a king nonetheless.

In John 18, Jesus comes out and says he is the king. Jesus came to set things right, to be a counselor, a mighty God, a prince of peace, an everlasting father.

Do you believe Jesus is your king? Do you joyfully submit to Jesus Christ as your prince, as your Lord? Does this affect your time, money, studies, body, mind, heart, or your plans in any way? What would it mean if Jesus really were treated as the king he is?

But how can you believe all of this? Isn't there some sort of sign? Yes.

The Bible tells us Jesus was born of a virgin.

In Matthew 1:18–25 we read:

> Now the birth of Jesus Christ took place in this way. When his mother Mary had been betrothed to Joseph, before they came together she was found to be with child from the Holy Spirit. And her husband Joseph, being a just man and unwilling to put her to shame, resolved to divorce her quietly. But as he considered these things, behold, an angel of the Lord appeared to him in a dream, saying, "Joseph, son of David, do not fear to take Mary as your wife, for that which is conceived in her is from the Holy Spirit. She will bear a son, and you shall call his name Jesus, for he will save his people from their sins." All this took place to fulfill what the Lord had spoken by the prophet:
>
> "Behold, the virgin shall conceive and bear a son, and they shall call his name Immanuel" (which means, God with us). When Joseph woke from sleep, he did as the angel of the Lord commanded him: he took his wife, but knew her not until she had given birth to a son. And he called his name Jesus.

You saw Isaiah 7 right there in the text, right? Matthew says this ancient prophecy applies to Jesus. Jesus' mother Mary was a virgin so this fulfills the Isaiah 7 prophecy.

The most important question today is to ask and possibly answer: "Who was and who is Jesus Christ?"

Many of you want to ask, "What does Christianity say about x?" Abortion. Politics. The death penalty. Gambling. Trump. Gay marriage. Racial reconciliation. Those are important questions, and we can have great discussions about these topics.

But those questions are not at the core of Christianity. The core, essential, bottom line question is "Who is Jesus?"

Just imagine what it would have been like to be Joseph asking this question. He found out his fiancé was pregnant. Who is the father? Uh... God is.

Right. People still try that excuse. It doesn't work.

Joseph hears this from Mary, and he's trying to treat her well, but he knows the birds and the bees. But then an angel visits him to deliver news, and he gets the prophecy from Isaiah 7, which he's heard before in Hebrew school.

This is the one, the Immanuel? It's hardly believable. The faith and trust of this young couple is intense—despairing, desperate, marginalized, confused, having a child this way. What will people think? Nine months of explanations in a high honor culture. Better to divorce her quietly and not have to deal with it.

But God tells him to have faith. He doesn't give him a twenty-page explanation of how this is going to work out. He says, "All you need to know is I will be with you. Trust me."

I will be with you. Immanuel.

This is truly a Nevertheless-Moment that comes out of an Ahaz Question. Joseph had to be tempted to handle this in the ways he knew, something that made far more sense than what he was being asked to do.

It is an unexpected light in the darkness. Would you expect the King of Kings and Lord of Lords, the Messiah, the Expected One, God-Made-Flesh to be born as a child, born in the dinkiest city, born to the poorest of parents, born in a cattle stall, born in a feed trough, born with only shepherds and animals around?

It's undignified. It's unsterile! It isn't very likely, distinguished, or celebratory. It is common, dirty, and dark. Stables are smelly places. They're full of stinky animals. It's rather humbling.

Christmas is about God With Us coming into the darkness in this humbling Nevertheless-Moment in your smelly stable without all the answers, because we cannot save ourselves. The real crisis is soul-killing, world-killing sin, and its destruction and lack of a desire for God. But God says, in just that situation, "I've come to do something about it. Trust me with your life."

Can you do that? Can you believe this sign is real, true, and accurate? We all have Ahaz scenarios where we scramble and try to make things work. We make alliances with powers around us. We make deals with our oppressors in some sort of a Stockholm Syndrome. We try to cope.

God says "Trust me. Follow me. I love you. I'm with you."

The ones who were at Jesus' birth were the shepherds, the least likely people to witness the birth of a king. If you are to come and follow Christ, you have to be the same. You have to come to him on your knees, acknowledging your unlikelihood to be loved, accepted, honored, and cherished. If you come to him demanding things because you deserve it, then you do not know him or his way.

Following Christ is not only humbling. It's scary.

It's like learning how to ride a bike. You have to trust it will work as you're riding it.

I taught my kids to ride their bikes when they were little. You know you are right, and they're convinced you're wrong. Adults have a difficult time remembering back to what it was like to ride for the first time. Even if you could remember, it is hard to explain.

The child can see his brother and sister riding their bikes. But he also can see if he lifts his legs right away while he's not moving, the bike will fall over. Somehow, staying up means moving, and that is petrifying.

Kids have to trust the design of the bike. They have to trust parents who tell them to pedal and steer and trust it will be okay even if they fall sometimes. They have to be humble and say their knowledge of the world wasn't all there is, to admit someone wiser might know more. It seems contrary to both emotion and reason.

It feels so much safer to have legs down on the ground than to pick them up. But there is so much more freedom to trust and pedal. You'll fly with freedom. It's impossible not to smile. The payoff is big.

There are areas of our life where we think we have to take matters into our own hands, aren't there? We're tired of waiting. We're not sure how it's going to turn out. We have Ahaz Moments, Ahaz Decisions, Ahaz Scenarios, and Ahaz Questions.

Some of you are married, and you're starting to say, "This is way harder than I thought. I've tried everything. I want out. I'm not trusting you any more God, I don't think any part of this could be redemptive." God says to trust and follow him and his ways.

Some of you desperately want to be married. Or just be in a relationship. Or to have been asked out. You want a relationship. You're thinking, "If I could just have that right person and get married then everything will be right." But you're tired of waiting.

So you lower your standards, and take whoever comes along. Even for just a little while. God says to trust and follow him and his ways.

Someday, after you've gotten your job or your house or your kids or your degree or your promotion or your membership or your—you know, the things you've always thought if you just had them, you'd be really happy—you'll find yourself awash with disappointment. Or bitterness. Or self pity. Or cynicism.

Those are Ahaz Moments. Those are fake kings and rulers in your life you've tried to serve. Those shoots only approximate the real thing. God says to trust and follow him and his ways.

Jesus' life, death, and resurrection all point to him being *the* Immanuel, God with us. That's what Christmas means. Not that you will create some sort of goodness or light out of your life, but there is goodness and light outside of you, and his name is Jesus. Jesus is God. God living and born among us. In the midst of all our despair, God has broken through and walked among us. Stake your life on this. Lean not on your own understanding.

The Bible claims this. Jesus claims this. His followers believed this, however impossible it seemed. The least likely people to believe did so.

Why?

Unexpected greatness.

Winston Zeddemore was asked if he believed in the paranormal. His response was, "If there's a steady paycheck in it, I'll believe in anything." That's how he was picked to be an original Ghostbuster.

Perhaps our greatest president, Abraham Lincoln, was a nobody. He came from common origins, was tall and homely with a high-pitched voice. He was a mass of contradictions because he was funny, depressed, lonely, humble, ambitious, and a visionary who made compromises. He lost more elections than he won. He suffered in his marriage. He lost multiple children.

Lincoln revered the founding fathers, but he knew slavery was a failure, and the stench of it was evil. He felt America itself was at stake, and he set out to convince a skeptical public with vision, determination, and perseverance. Lincoln believed God's woe was cast upon our nation because of this slavery.

In the midst of incredible chaos and unsurety, Lincoln spoke these words at his Second Inaugural Address:

Fondly do we hope, fervently do we pray, that this mighty scourge of war may speedily pass away. Yet, if God wills that it continue until all the wealth piled by the bondsman's two hundred and fifty years of unrequited toil shall be sunk, and until every drop of blood drawn with the lash shall be paid by another drawn with the sword, as was said three thousand years ago, so still it must be said "the judgments of the Lord are true and righteous altogether." With malice toward none, with charity for all, with firmness in the right as God gives us to see the right, let us strive on to finish the work we are in, to bind up the nation's wounds, to care for him who shall have borne the battle and for his widow and his orphan, to do all which may achieve and cherish a just and lasting peace among ourselves and with all nations.[10]

700,000 American died in that Civil War. It came at a great cost to set some things right. To give liberty and justice for all. We still have work to do.

There is an unexpected greatness to that man. Mark Robinson is the the president of Antioch College, He counts Abraham Lincoln as one of his heroes, and rightly so. He ends his TED talk[11] on Lincoln by telling his audience we cannot all be great. But we can walk with the great. We can stand with them, support them, and follow them.

Our Christmas question—no matter what time of year you're reading this— is "Who is Jesus?"

How great was he? And will you walk with him?

If he really is God among us, then you need to give yourself to him and all he has for you to do.

If you aren't sure, then you need to study and pursue this with all your heart.

Perhaps for the first time you can believe in and receive the light. Perhaps again, for you have forgotten out of pride or unbelief or self-ishness or despair.

He has given you signs. Will you believe them or not? If Jesus is really born of a virgin, it might be true he is Wonderful Counselor,

Mighty God, Everlasting Father, Prince of Peace. It just might be true he is God. John 1 might be true. Wouldn't that be great if it were true? Wouldn't that make more sense than the random firings of the synapses in your brain causing these jumpings in your heart?

Will you take your feet off the ground and begin to experience freedom or keep the training wheels on? This is the nature of faith and belief.

There is a child born of a virgin who is the ideal ruler from the root of Jesse. His name is Jesus Christ. He is Immanuel, God with us. Come to him.

ISAIAH 24–25

Julie and I (Doug) have lived in the Oklahoma City area since 2001, and we've seen amazing changes. OKC is a great place to live, and it's getting better. We're seeing new developments, restaurants, business ventures, city parks, white water rapids, and streetcars.

No one would confuse OKC with a world-class or first-class city. We've got a long way to go. We've made mistakes, and our city's amenities aren't accessible to everyone. We're too tied to oil and gas. We're too racially divided. Our politics, schools, and budgets are a mess.

But we've made great strides. We've come a long way since the late 80s and early 90s. We've been through tragedy together. We've taken risks. We've come a long way and still have a long way left to go.

Different cities. Think about where you live or where you've visited. Denver, LA, Albuquerque, Toronto, Branson, Seattle, Tokyo—all different, and all important.

Isaiah was written sometime in the 700s BC. 1,100 years afterward, St. Augustine of Hippo wrote a book called *The City of God* while Rome was sacked by the Goths in 410 AD.

Rome fell! That had seemed impossible.

Augustine wrestled with the theological implications of his crumbling world. In his book, he proposes all people inhabit one of two cities, either the city of man or the city of God. Though people may all be different—DNA, eras, places, ethnicities—the city of Man is unified *against* God. Humanity builds its own world on its own terms. The city of God, however weak and disparate it seems at times, will not fail. It doesn't look like it's going to win the day, but God invites all of us to pack up and move to that greatest of cities because the address will welcome you, and it will last forever.

Isaiah 24 and 25 reveal to us a little bit more about greatness, but this time we'll be talking about great cities. Let's look and see what God can show us, and let's consider which city we have citizenship in.

The City of Man

Our main verse for this first point is one of judgment found in Isaiah 24:10: *"The wasted city is broken down; every house is shut up so that none can enter."*

To get to that point, look back over where we left off with Isaiah 11 when we saw there would be a root from the stump of Jesse. There needs to be a root, because things aren't going so well in the city of man after all.

If you merely scan the topics and headings in your Bible through the next fourteen chapters (11 through 25), you'll see judgments and oracles concerning Philistia, Moab, Damascus, Cush, Egypt, Tyre, and Sidon. You'll see signs against Egypt, Cush, and Babylon.

You'll even see Jerusalem in the mix. That's a lot closer to home. The nations and cities of the world are being judged, and they're all found wanting, including Jerusalem.

What's the problem? Why not start with a clean slate? Why does God have to be so judgmental?

Look at Isaiah 14:12ff. It's an excellent example of what we're talking about, what God's dealing with. This is one of the judgments as God assesses Babylon which was a great nation, one of the superpowers of the day. In the Ancient Near East, the major players of the region went from Assyria to Babylon to Greece to Rome.

But God looks at these cultures differently. He cuts down those who ascend to heaven above the stars. We attempt to make our own Camelot or Mount Olympus, but God will judge our pride and arrogance. We do great things, but all within our context of greatness. There's a sense where everything we do is relative, but we think we are the absolute gold standard. God says otherwise.

He can—and will—bring us low. He created us, and he can take us out. He can take us to Sheol. We actually deserve to go. His holiness is not relative at all. We've all failed. We've all fallen short. We've all sinned. So this judgment should not be that surprising.

And yet it is. We want more credit than we deserve. Compared to Hitler or Saddam or Jeffrey Dahmer or Timothy McVeigh, we consider ourselves saints. It's relatively true.

God's assessment is different.

None of us are holy. We're all incredibly broken, even the best and greatest of us. God's holiness requires him to rise up against unholiness. He cannot take injustice. He cannot let go of abuse or theft or manipulation. His ways and judgments are just.

So the destiny of this city in Isaiah 14 is under the judgment of God. Its drunken songs cannot push away or mask the sadness.

Things could be different but for the pride of man. Look at how this oracle describes it in Isaiah 16:6:

> We have heard of the pride of Moab—how proud he is!—of his arrogance, his pride, and his insolence; in his idle boasting he is not right.

Pride works this way. It's considered the worst of the Seven Deadly Sins, the root of them all. It goes all the way back to the Garden of Eden, when Adam and Eve believed Satan, and they thought they knew best. They said God could no longer be trusted.

We know pride goes before the fall, but we still think highly of ourselves not only when we do well but also when things go against us. It's always someone else's fault. We're always a victim of circumstances, and we give ourselves the benefit of the doubt.

Even our despair can be rooted in pride. We don't want to turn to help. We'd rather go it alone and do it ourselves. Meritocracy is strong, whether we achieve and succeed or fail and fall flat on our faces. Pride helps us keep sailing above the surface of our lives so we can remain unaware of the depths that lie below.

Pride can look like Kanye loving him some Kanye, Doug some

Doug, or Matt some Matty Matt. We can take pride in our goodness, morals, rebelliousness, beauty, lack of exercise, bad grades, perfect attendance, sloppy appearance, frugality, urban consciousness, progressive liberalism, duty to country, or our growing achievements.

We're also often proud of not liking something popular. We take stands against the Super Bowl or Hamilton or Katy Perry.[1]

We're proud of our cynicism, as if it's some admirable quality to always see through everything.

We're somehow proud that we no longer get shocked by things. We've seen violence so much it's no longer horrifying. Our knowledge has not translated into responsibility. We keep walking, keep clicking, and keep distant. We explain evil away over and over and over, without tears or empathy. We're wise to the world. We've been around.

We're proud that we can offend and confuse others. We're happy when we strike nerves. We're thrilled when something we say or do is considered shocking and vulgar.

We're proud when we're on the right side (so we think) of a social media shaming mob.

We're proud that we're getting older and wiser, which we are supposed to do, but we think it's some amazing attribute or quality as if people "these days" are getting worse and worse.

We're somehow proud of succeeding without doing any work, waking up in a stranger's bed, sleeping in past noon, the street signs we've stolen, of cooking box Mac and Cheese.

I was reading about both successful and doomed companies, and if there's any way to tell if a CEO is truly giving back to his shareholders, investors, employees, and customers, or if the CEO is faking it to get ahead. Is there a way to tell if he or she is a giver or a taker? One focus was on the CEO of Enron, Kenneth Lay. It's hard to remember he was incredibly influential, the epitome of the rich and famous.

He was a taker. Over and over again, everything was all about him —the money, fame, accolades, power, vacations, salary. One indication of this was a simple one: his picture on the yearly report kept getting bigger and bigger. It was like Enron was all about him.

Enron went bankrupt in 2001. Over 20,000 people lost their jobs and many of them their life savings. Investors lost billions of dollars. Lay was charged and convicted with ten counts of fraud in 2006, and he died before his sentencing.

Pride did not forever go unpunished. It led to a whole lot of harm for people. Pride was not only personal for Lay. It affected thousands and thousands of other people.

The point is God will judge the city of man. Isaiah writes:

> "I will rise up against them," declares the Lord of hosts, "and will cut off from Babylon name and remnant, descendants and posterity," declares the Lord. "And I will make it a possession of the hedgehog, and pools of water, and I will sweep it with the broom of destruction," declares the Lord of hosts. (Isa. 15:22)

Hear Isaiah's haunting imagery as he describes what it will be like on that day:

> The earth mourns and withers; the world languishes and withers; the highest people of the earth languish. The earth lies defiled under its inhabitants, for they have transgressed the laws, violated the statutes, broken the everlasting covenant. Therefore a curse devours the earth, and its inhabitants suffer for their guilt; therefore the inhabitants of the earth are scorched, and few men are left. The wine mourns, the vine languishes, all the merry-hearted sigh. The mirth of the tambourines is stilled, the noise of the jubilant has ceased, the mirth of the lyre is stilled. No more do they drink wine with singing; strong drink is bitter to those who drink it. The wasted city is broken down; every house is shut up so that none can enter. There is an outcry in the streets for lack of wine; all joy has grown dark; the gladness of the earth is banished. Desolation is left in the city; the gates are battered into ruins.
>
> For thus it shall be in the midst of the earth among the nations, as when an olive tree is beaten, as at the gleaning when the grape harvest is done. (Isa. 24:4–13)

We come back to our assessment summary sentence in Isaiah 24:10: "The wasted city is broken down; every house is shut up so that none can enter."

The wasted city is broken down.

Back before God formed the world, Genesis 1:2 describes the

scene this way: *"The earth was without form and void, and darkness was over the face of the deep."* Formless and void. Dark. Broken down. God's judgment on the city of man brings us back to a formless, voided, dark space. The mythology of human pride is exposed, the defiant plastic artificiality is burned away, and our precariously phony lives will be revealed for what they are.

There's a day coming when we won't worry about what Beyonce says, what the president tweets, the Dow, oil prices, or what's happening in the next draft. That day is coming.

To our modern ears, this sounds awful. And it is! But I want to remind you this happens all the time, albeit on a much smaller scale.

We're trying to redo our church's courtyard back into a gathering space. Many years ago, it was a lawn with green grass in front of the church. We have pictures of the building looking like this. At some point, someone ripped out the sod and bushes and replaced it with asphalt to make a parking lot.

We planted two trees to jump-start this process. We had to rip up the pavement. We cut two squares and dug deep. We created a pile of debris, so something new could be planted. In doing so, we judged the asphalt plan a bad one. We're not mad at the people who made that decision, but going a new direction inherently means making a decision about the old one. Planting something new means going against something old. It creates a mess, a void. That formless void of a hole only lasted a few hours, but it had to be made nonetheless.

That same idea is true all over each city and the world. We can reclaim old properties. Still, in doing so, we have to go in a new direction. Sometimes we raze a whole site and start from scratch. We tear down buildings and blocks in order to build new buildings or parks. We leave a structure standing, but we gut it and give it something totally new inside.

We make mistakes in doing this. We get it wrong.

But God doesn't. He's the perfect, righteous judge. He gets it right. He's at work in the other city, the city of God.

The City of God

I'm trying to get you to see that any change requires some sort of judgment call. If we're going to go in a new direction, we're saying the old direction was not working. If we change the channel, we're eliminating one for another.

I'm mesmerized by one of the chapters in the *This American Life* episode "Fermi's Paradox." The episode was about being alone, and this chapter dealt with marriage. It focused on a marriage counselor who records her sessions and plays them with permission. She's dealing with a couple that seemingly had a great marriage, but a bombshell was dropped that the husband had been cheating on the wife for twenty-two years.

In the session, therapist Esther Perel keeps helping them talk to each other, and especially coaching the husband listen to his wife. She says over and over again, "Don't do it that way. Try this."

He tries, it helps, and it works. Esther redirects. She shuts him down. She stops him. He starts to get what she's saying. He and his wife start connecting.

Judgment of the wrong way helps get to the right way. Esther Perel wants the couple to have hope that something can be different, that freedom can come, and trust reborn. But not by continuing in the same ways, patterns, and dysfunctions.

One more example: We talked last chapter about the stumps of Jesse, the deforestation of what used to be a healthy ecosystem. A while back a church member, two deacons, and an elder at City Pres embarked on an ambitious stumpy project. They started cutting down the mulberry tree in our courtyard.

I have nothing against mulberry trees per se. I'm sure they serve a good purpose.

However, this one particular tree would rain down thousands and thousands of mulberries each for a month often right around Easter. They'd cover a large section of our courtyard, and there was no way to get rid of them all. So for at least a month, Sundays were filled with smeared, smashed mulberries all over the church carpet and on kids' clothes and across their mouths (they ate a *ton* of them).

That tree had to go. It was an easy judgment call, but a judgment call nonetheless. We climbed, hacked, and sawed away, filling up a dumpster with limbs. So now we have our own stump, our own picture of God's judgment, of what was not good, not best, not what we wanted.

But... heaven is coming! Isaiah 24:1 calls us to look and behold at what destruction lies around us, so we do. But we also want to notice the grace and mercy of God as he builds his heavenly city. The text itself calls for hope and encouragement in the midst of the chaos.

Isaiah 12 is a totally different vibe:

You will say in that day: "I will give thanks to you, O Lord, for though you were angry with me, your anger turned away, that you might comfort me. Behold, God is my salvation; I will trust, and will not be afraid; for the Lord God is my strength and my song, and he has become my salvation." With joy you will draw water from the wells of salvation. And you will say, in that day: "Give thanks to the Lord, call upon his name, make known his deeds among his peoples, proclaim that his name is exalted. Sing praises to the Lord, for he has done gloriously; let this be made known in all the earth. Shout, and sing for joy, O inhabitant of Zion, for great in your midst is the Holy One of Israel."

And Isaiah 14:1:

For the Lord will have compassion on Jacob and will again choose Israel, and will set them in their own land, and sojourners will join them and will attach themselves to the house of Jacob.

And Isaiah 16:3-5:

Give counsel; grant justice; make your shade like night at the height of noon; shelter the outcasts; do not reveal the fugitive; let the outcasts of Moab sojourn among you; be a shelter to them from their destroyer. When the oppressor is no more and destruction has ceased, and he who tramples underfoot is vanished from the land, then a throne will be established in steadfast love, and on it will sit in faithfulness in the tent of David one who judges and seeks justice and is swift to do righteousness.

While Esther Perel is in a session with a couple, she is honing in not only on what they're doing and saying wrong. She's encouraging something else, some bright spots, some hope that there can be a connection, an idea that even in a short amount of time there can be a shift and change into a different space of wholeness, integrity, trust, and intimacy.

I remember standing in the middle of a rundown, old, worn out, seemingly useless building in OKC called Sunshine Cleaners. My friends Jon, Ben, and David threw a party not for what was, but for what could be, for what *would* be. They had a vision for something coming out of that rubble, for a new building built from the ashes. They saw something in those bones of Sunshine Cleaners. They put time and effort into resurrecting it to be even better than it ever was. They honored that building by reclaiming it. Now you can go get a beer at StoneCloud Brewery.

We're used to these apocalyptic visions in our movies. We've seen a vision of the world ruined from atom bombs, aliens, machines, and zombies.

A few weeks ago, we watched *The Matrix* because my youngest daughter Anna hadn't seen it. Talk about a vision of destruction!

And yet, there is a resistance, a remnant—Zion, the city that still remains. And there's a chosen one, the one who will lead the people to defeat the enemy.

And so we turn to Isaiah 25!

This gets personal. Isaiah starts out, *"O Lord, you are my God. I will exalt you; I will praise your name, for you have done wonderful things, plans formed of old, faithful and sure"* (Isa. 25:1).

This isn't an intellectual exercise, a philosophy class, or even a theological seminar. It matters to him. He's making declarations and statements, but he's exalting, singing, and proclaiming God's goodness to himself and others. He's personally involved.

God is building a new city, and this one is on the mountain of the Lord. All are invited. It's not for one particular type of person, language, or ethnicity. It's for all who make it there. God's at work building this city. He's not spreading everyone out in the suburbs or the countryside. He's building a new city of grace.

We can often and easily talk about city evils—crime, injustice, corruption, abuse, etc. But we also need to remember cities are where we get culture, intellectual ideas, help, care, and progress. We learn about each other in the city. We share collective triumphs.

What makes a great city?[2]

Great cities have cultural assets that are open and accessible to everyone. Those are interesting, invigorating, and connected. There's a buy-in from everyone, which means a cultural and ethnic diversity. There are big ticket items but a million small contributions from local artists, musicians, chefs, and entrepreneurs. People don't feel isolated. Sprawl is minimized, and connectivity is maximized. Pollution and crime are kept low. People need to and want to feel safe and secure. That's important. A great city has natural assets and green spaces. Great cities have common spaces, walk-ability, and bike-ability. People want to spend time outdoors, whether that means on boulevards, river walks, hiking trails, fountains, or tourist sites. Great cities foster sustainable, civil societies.

Great cities build cool, accessible places that are for everyone. There is access. That means justice and not injustice. Police but not over-policing. There's something about a great city in how it treats the poor and needy with buses, schools, food, space, and services.

At least that's what the Bible says. Isaiah writes:

For you have been a stronghold to the poor, a stronghold to the needy in his distress, a shelter from the storm and a shade from the heat; for the breath of the ruthless is like a storm against a wall, like heat in a dry place. (Isa. 25:4–5)

How does the city of God treat "the least of these"? How does the city of God treat the orphans, widows, the poor, and the poor in spirit?

Well, the city of God is no respecter of persons. All will be judged. All will be laid low. Kings and queens will be right alongside everyone else. God will judge the VIPs and dignitaries.

And he'll raise up the lowly.

God says there will be an amazingly great free buffet you've stumbled onto. You didn't even have to pay for it but someone did. You might be a wedding crasher, but you ended up at the right place at the right time. The greatest chef in the world has set out a spread of the best food and wine and the most sumptuous feast, and it's all free to you.

Some of the best free meals I've been to have been at weddings. I've eaten a five-course meal in the Catskill Mountains. I've eaten Memphis barbecue and Louisiana gumbo. I've saddled up to the bar for premium gin and tonics. It did cost me because I had to be there. I invested the time in the relationship to that point. I'd had both good and difficult conversations, and I often wondered where things were going. And the wedding, vows, dance, and the feast was glorious. Everyone there ate the same good food because they were connected to the couple. There was no distinction. All you had to do was to be there and participate.

Urbanist Joel Kotkin writes:

> The three major characteristics of great cities are that they are sacred, safe, and busy. Whether Tenochtitlan, New York City, Paris or any other great city of the world, you will find these characteristics.[3]

Sacred. Safe. Busy.

So all who are connected to God are welcome. That's the requirement to get to Zion, to the mountain of the Lord, to be able to taste and see that the Lord is good.

You've got to be able to honestly say, *"Behold, this is our God; we have waited for him, that he might save us. This is the Lord; we have waited for him; let us be glad and rejoice in his salvation"* (Isa. 25:9). This is our God. We've waited for him that he might save us. This is the Lord. Let's be glad! Let's rejoice in his salvation!

There may be some reasons to say, "Where have you been? What took so long?" But more important is to be there and rejoice that God came at all.

He's come to save! Since we need saving, this is a fantastic arrangement. We need God. We've waited, and he's arrived, even though he didn't have to. He's saving desperately needy, wicked people like you and me. We've broken the covenant, and yet he's paid the price so we can be at the extravagant party. He's working to take care of all the cost, tears, injustice, and all the brokenness.

It sounds like a party I want to attend. How about you?

Sacred. Safe. Busy. Accessible. Connected with buy-in.

All that futility will be eradicated. The city of God will be different than the city of man. Tears will be wiped away. Justice will rule. We'll break out of the spells of our matrices, our illusions of pride, and our towers of Babel to the sky. We'll know what's really important and what we can pass through and by. Pompous pride will be done away with, trampled like dunghills. Credit will be honest and accurate, going to the real heroes instead of the fake CEOs. We won't just keep swimming away. We'll be carried on the tide of God's grace and mercy.

Isaiah says the covering will be done away with, the veil will be lifted, and the death pall will be eradicated. Death will be swallowed up forever! ALS, cancer, strokes, traffic accidents, Alzheimers, leukemia—done.

I'm still haunted by my friend Dustin. He was riding his bike with his boys in his cul-de-sac. His bike slipped, he hit the ground, and he hit his head. Nothing dangerous happened, but still he went into a coma, and he died several months later.

Why?

My uncle served in the Navy in Vietnam in a submarine. He died from asbestos poisoning from the close quarters and months in the submarine. That doesn't seem just.

Children die from diseases they got from their moms and dads.

The world is a brutal place. Evolution and natural selection say, "Eh." That's the way of sorting the strong and the weak.

God says, "This is not the way it's supposed to be. I will change things. Look for a better day."

And he says even more: *"He will swallow up death forever"* (Isa. 25:8).

Sounds like a miracle cure. Like maybe wearing copper bracelets will be the answer, or a guru has found the secret to eternal life. All we have to do is send in money, believe in him, and never go to the doctor again.

But Jesus Christ, the Chosen One, was predicted by the oracles in Isaiah 7, 9 and 11. He says he is the way, the truth, and the life. He says he is the resurrection and the life. He's said he will provide eternal life for all who believe in and enter into him.

There have been others who have claimed to have discovered eternal life—Ziusudra. Tithonus. Achilles, Ino, Helen, Tithonus, and more. The Wandering Jew. John the Apostate. The Three Nephites. Sir Galahad and Merlin.

And Jesus Christ, of Nazareth, born of a virgin, the forever ruler from the root of Jesse.

What do you think? The Bible says Jesus was the Chosen One, the Messiah, the King of Kings and Lord of Lords, the firstborn of all creation, God himself, the second person of the Trinity, very God of very God, begotten and not made, born of the virgin Mary, suffered under Pontius Pilate, was crucified, buried, descended into hell, and was raised on the third day, from there to judge the living and dead. And he will return.

So the Scriptures teach us Jesus conquered death by dying. That's counterintuitive. The weak shall be strong. The poor shall be rich. Blessed are those who hunger and thirst for righteousness. All my righteousness is filthy rags. All my wisdom is foolishness. The city of God is upside down. Things are not all as they appear. You can get set free from the sunken place. You can re-enter reality in Christ.

The Bible says there's a really strange, amazing banquet up ahead in this new city. It's the body and blood of Christ, which means its super relational and also weirdly transformational. I can't explain it all, just like I can't fully describe all of Isaiah 25.

What will a city and world without tears or sin or injustice look like? You tell me. All I know is that it's not going to look like what we have here,

Death will be swallowed up. Injustice will be set right. Yours and mine. Ours. Our sins we've committed that we know about and those we don't. The ones we did on purpose, and the things we left undone that we should have done. Our good intentions will be exposed too.

We've got a choice to make. This might all be hogwash. Or there might be a different Neo, Messiah, or Chosen One. Or Jesus Christ of Nazareth might be the real deal. Of course, he may not be.

Buddha didn't think so. As much as he respected Jesus, Mohammed didn't trust in him.

Maybe there is a place where we can thrive. Maybe it will be a beautiful, prosperous, sustainable, just, true, good, well-ordered city. Maybe we could go there someday.

Jesus says we can. He says he's preparing a place, and if we're united to him, we'll find that place, that life, those relationships. Perhaps oddly, the entryway citizenship to that city resides in a relationship with him, with Jesus. We can't earn our way there. We can't buy our way in. We can't outsmart it or outwork it. There's no secret tunnel or papers or underground railroad. We have to go in with him, united to him.

He will swallow up death forever?

Jesus said, *"I am the resurrection and the life"* (John 11:25). Jesus submitted to death.

So now we have an Easter sermon. Our previous texts were about Christmas, and we're here now at Easter. We're reading about trampling under the greatest foe, death itself. We're talking about conquering death because death itself is dying. We're talking about new life, creations, cities, and new freedom in this banquet of salvation.

In Christ, we look forward to being forever united to him and living in the new heavens and the new earth, the new city, the city of God! O death, where is your sting?! In the city of man, we're living for ourselves. We're rebels against God and his ways. In the city of God, we're living for God, and we're rebels against ourselves and our prideful ways.

In which city do you live? In which city do you hope to live? Perhaps, as Paul says, all things are really rubbish, and to live is Christ, and to die is gain.

Melody Warnick wondered about what makes people love the city they live in. What roots them there so they know they belong? Studies show it usually takes an average of four to five years before someone feels that belonging sense of place. She wondered if she might be able to jump-start that by practicing placemaking principles from the very beginning of arriving in a new city, in this case Blacksburg, Virginia. Her book *This Is Where You Belong* details that art/science project.

Her list of practices to truly love her place are: walk more, buy local, get to know my neighbors, do fun stuff, explore nature, volunteer, eat local, become more political, create something new, and stay loyal through hard times.

I live in a great city. I love it here. I love the people, amenities, culture, food, parks, theaters, and neighborhoods. I love reading about people I know in the paper when they're doing great things in our city. It's satisfying being involved in what's going on at Harding Charter Prep, Thelma Parks, and The Academy. I appreciate the Plaza District, the Plaza Walls murals, and the shrimp and grits with a local IPA at Oak and Ore. I work on sermons at Urban Tea House, the Sip, Uppercrust, and McNellies. I love the new streetcars and all the advancements with the MAPS projects. I eat soul food on the Northeast side with Pastor Michael. I'm thankful that City Pres sits in the middle of a diverse culture, a crossroads of people, and I pray more will find their way to this space where God reigns, so we can thrive together.

I don't live in the greatest city in the world, but I don't want to be anywhere else. Perhaps I could practice more ideas from Melody Warnick's list.

In fact, we could do that for the city of God too. We live there already, and yet we don't all the way yet. We look forward to more, so let's be practicing those habits and disciplines now. Let's be the city of God we want to be. Let's walk more with Jesus. Let's get to know our neighbors. Let's throw great parties. Let's explore, eat from the Lord's table, get involved, create new things, and stay loyal through hard times, may they come again no more.

I pray we'll be reminded of the city of God. I pray we'll all be invited there, and we'll put away the city of man. The city of God is one of true grace and beauty, mercy and justice coming together on the cross. We're brought together, unified by the blood of Christ, so we can run and play in his great city.

Behold, this is our God! We look forward to what he's doing as we walk up to his mountain to be with him at the glorious wedding supper banquet of the Lamb of God It will be sacred, safe, and busy in his gracious salvation.

ISAIAH 26

Rachel Howard won't watch *Law & Order*, won't play Clue, and she won't attend murder mystery dinners.

In 1986, Rachel's father Stan was murdered while she slept in the next room. She spent the next fifteen years dealing with in the only way she knew how—she pretended it never happened.

She's written a book about her experience in working through this still-unsolved murder, *The Lost Night*. In an interview on *This American Life*,[1] she talked about how people deal with their grief. Most people start an unending quest to find the killer and bring that person to justice.

Rachel did the same thing. She investigated it on her own for years—talking to police, tracking down files, submitting requests for information, and so on. At the end of her work, she asked a crime reporter to look at what she had compiled.

He did.

And he told her she should give up.

He'd seen hundreds of cases like this, and he didn't think the murderer would ever be found.

Rachel loved her dad. She misses him. Everyone loses parents, but this is a tragic, terrible way for it to happen.

In *The Atlantic Monthly*, Eric Schlosser wrote:

Americans are fascinated by murder and murderers, but not by the families of people who are killed. One might expect that the families of murder victims would be showered with sympathy and support, embraced by their communities. But in reality, they're far more likely to feel isolated, fearful, and ashamed, overwhelmed by grief and guilt.[2]

Rachel gave up, and in doing, so she felt free and liberated. She's trusting something else now, some other way to find peace for her grief.

The Bible surely knows grief. It's not shy about naming and describing the reality of living in our fallen, broken world.

You don't have to know much about the setting of Isaiah to think of how things might have been in the Ancient Near East in the 700s BC. Life was difficult. Women died in childbirth all the time every day. Few children made it to adulthood. Kids worked. Houses were tiny, dark, and dirty. Death was everywhere. An army could show up at any point and either kill everyone or make those captured their slaves.

This is the way people lived for most of human history. Think of the trials and hardships of Indigenous Americans, the pilgrims, the settlers and explorers, or the Boomers and Sooners. Think of life without running water and indoor plumbing. Think about life before cell phones—the dark ages!

But what about now? Our life expectancies are high. Our freedoms are amazing. For the most part, our disposable income is steady and growing.

Yet, we're still afraid. We're still human and feel fragile. We're depressed, and we work too much. We have not solved grief by any means. We've canceled out many illnesses and diseases, but new ones have cropped up (including the one we're not talking about), and it never seems to end. There is still war, chaos, rioting, violence, human trafficking, and slavery.

Even without those big ones, we feel disconnected and disintegrated. In Chuck DeGroat's book *Wholeheartedness*, researcher Brigid Schulte puts it this way:

This is how it feels to live my life: scattered, fragmented, and exhausting. I am always doing more than one thing at a time and feel I never do any one particularly well. I'm always behind and always late, with one more thing and one more thing and one more thing to do before rushing out the door. Entire hours evaporate—while I'm doing stuff that needs to get done. But once I'm done, I can't tell you what it was I did or why it seemed so important.[3]

So this is a lot of #firstworldproblems, but saying that doesn't seem to help us not worry about them. We're a stressed out, anxious, depressed group of people. Scattered, fragmented, and exhausted.

So could ancient words have anything to say to our modern world, and our modern problems?

No Peace

On the one hand, everyone living in Isaiah's world would have a vested interest in the politics and news of the day. It mattered that Rome had been (legendarily) founded by Romulus and Remus a few decades before. The Ancient Greek Olympics weren't on TV, but these games made a difference in the spirit of the day. The Assyrian kings and queens were important. The Babylonians were splitting off and forming their own alliances. People wanted to know who this king was, how long he would last, and what type of rule he'd institute.

News sources were slow. So you may have very little warning that everything was about to change, the enemy was at the gate, the famine had arrived, or the sickness was spreading.

On the other hand, daily life was all-consuming. What will you eat today, and is anyone trying to eat you? How can we keep sickness away? Will we get chosen for marriage, and when, and to whom? Where am I going to sleep? When will I wash? Think of life without glasses, clean water, comfort food, or personal hygiene.

Peace was tough to get then, and it is now. The circumstances are different today all over the world—Canada, Haiti, Australia, or Nigeria. We're not all living the same lives, even today. We've made serious advancements, but people are still hungry, homeless, marginalized, mistreated, illiterate, and considered less than human in many places. We still have the politics of power and war. We struggle with peace, thinking it's just around the corner.

Bombs are going off. People are driving trucks into tourists, shooting their coworkers, bombing clinics, taking sex trips for under-aged girls, and getting hooked on meth. People are in jail in numbers that stagger the mind—in America.

We need help. We have to go in a new direction. We need an intervention. They did then, and we do now.

So we can look to Isaiah to help give us guidance, for a pattern of words and images for our heart's cries. We know this world isn't the way it's supposed to be. We know something has to be different. We may have more information at our disposal, but that means we might be smarter, more subtle sinners.

Isaiah writes:

> *O Lord, your hand is lifted up, but they do not see it. Let them see your zeal for your people, and be ashamed. Let the fire for your adversaries consume them....*
> *O Lord our God, other Lords besides you have ruled over us, but your name alone we bring to remembrance. They are dead, they will not live; they are shades, they will not arise, to that end you have visited them with destruction and wiped out all remembrance of them.* (Isa. 26:11, 13–14)

We remain positive, but we have to be honest and admit we want and need God to come through to judge what is evil. We're not only hoping for, praying for, and working for unicorns and rainbows. We need death, evil, and sickness to be done away with.

That means we need to be able to accurately identify death, evil, and sickness. One of our problems is we call what is good evil and what is evil good. We've got so many things so mixed up. I feel like I've (Doug) gotten to a place in my life and ministry when I can walk into darkness and fear no evil. I can go to dark places with Jesus. But not if the person says the dark is light, the night is day, and the evil is good—that's messed up. That's an alternate universe, a fake world.

We've mixed up God's views with our American culture. We add in our own specifics: White, Black, Hispanic, men, and women. Upper, middle, and lower class. Our modern idea of a Declaration of

Independence. Our personal story, good or bad. Our political views.
Our education level.

We live lives so connected to our own worldview, and of course
that makes sense to us. It's entirely natural, and we don't often pause
to consider how differently we'd think if we were born to a different
family, another skin color, the other gender, or a century ahead or
behind, or on the other side of the world.

We need to see God's hand lifted up, to see what he sees. That
may be to our shame, but if it's true then it's good.

The sad truth is we've all followed other rulers and leaders. We've
had other lords and lovers in our lives. It may be Safety. Security.
Achievement. Easy Street. Do It Myself. Adrenaline. Significance.

Maybe the best example or illustration would be to have picked
the wrong person to marry. It made sense at the time. Perhaps you
didn't have all the information you do now. Things changed. You
were duped. You did the best you could, but now it feels like you
wasted all those years, tears, time, conversations, and energy. He left
you high and dry. She took off. She went crazy. He never got better.

You were attached to something that ended up harming you. You
followed someone who was going the wrong way. Your loyalty ended
up being bad instead of good. You probably stuck it out longer then
you should have with a lover who didn't love you back.

Isaiah uses another graphic example when he writes:

> *Like a pregnant woman who writhes and cries out in her pangs when she is near
> to giving birth, so were we because of you, O Lord; we were pregnant, we
> writhed, but we have given birth to wind. We have accomplished no deliverance
> in the earth, and the inhabitants of the world have not fallen.* (Isa. 26:17–19)

I don't know many pregnant women who love being pregnant.
But what if you went through the whole nine months and there was
no baby?!

Only wind.

All that inconvenience, discomfort, and pain to give birth to nothing? That sounds terrible—no baby. Sadly, many know all too well
from miscarriage or stillbirth the picture Isaiah paints. Your baby is
more than wind, but Isaiah uses the description of suffocating loss to

say Israel was attached to a hope that could not be delivered. We need a deliverer. Isaiah says it will come in the form of a baby.

We need God to work. We need a judge. Rachel Howard does. She needs someone somewhere at some time to bring justice for her father. She may not get it in this life, but she has to hope all is not lost.

The Dalai Lama says, "Do not let the behavior of others destroy your inner peace." Some will tell you the most effective way to create peace in the world is to start with yourself. Then you make sure not to let others affect you. It's why meditating for several hours every day works. It's how we stay balanced, mindful, calm and grounded, especially in chaotic times.

Isaiah has a different message:

> Come, my people, enter your chambers, and shut your doors behind you; hide yourselves for a little while until the fury has passed by. For behold, the Lord is coming out from his place to punish the inhabitants of the earth for their iniquity, and the earth will disclose the blood shed on it, and will no more cover its slain. (Isa. 26:20–21)

Peace

Julie Teahan[4] writes about how she's decided to enter the chaos. For years and years she strived to achieve that work-life balance working moms are supposed to have. Maybe even what the Dalai Lama would advocate for. She tried to disconnect from work when she was at home and felt herself always wondering if she was missing an important call on her Blackberry. She'd try to be present at home or focused at her meetings, and always felt like things were reversed. In the end she felt like she was failing both work and family.

She writes:

> Here I am in 2017 and after some grey hairs and self-imposed anxiety, I have an announcement. I can't do it. I cannot separate work and life. It cannot be done and wait for it… my company now knows this and understands. Not only do they understand, they are giving staff the flexibility to deal with this reality…. Stop fixating on the figurative

scales of your life. Stop counter-balancing and measuring who gets what and what gets more. Stop trying to compartmentalize and divide. It is a fruitless exercise. Instead, accept that every day you will be making adjustments in order to accomplish all the roles you fulfill. A little to the left. A little to the right. Up. Down. Sideways. You will never be finished making these adjustments. That's life.[5]

I'm trying to give you some hooks so you can see I'm not only talking about the worst of circumstances with death and destruction, though that is probably what was on the mind of Isaiah when he wrote chapter 26. Death was always at the door.

But we can also find peace with a house full of teenage girls, four kids in a small house, siblings at home for summer break, studying for the bar exam, fear of being out of control, or when we're filled with envy, depression, anxiety, lack of contentment, and just about anything.

Ignoring it is not the way forward. We have to hope in something more and something bigger.

God says we shouldn't delve into ourselves, but we should trust in him. Isaiah writes:

> You keep him in perfect peace whose mind is stayed on you, because he trusts in you. Trust in the Lord forever, for the Lord God is an everlasting rock. (Isa. 26:3)

The Dalai Lama isn't all wrong. We should meditate. Christians call that prayer. And it should be a long time. It should be all day long, for we're to pray without ceasing.

Prayer is a conversation with God, and we have long prayers, short ones, spontaneous ones, written out thoughtful ones, and just about any time of talking you can think of. We come to him with all we've got. The work-life balance is to admit we don't have any balance, so we need God to help us. We trust in him for our finances, employees, grades, projects, health, kids and grandkids, safety, marriages, singleness, nation, politics, sins, and our freedoms—our everything.

We're not trusting in ourselves, as if when we delve into our inner person, we find something truly great. We trust in the Lord, the everlasting rock of our salvation. He loves us more than we can ever love him.

That's our great hope. God is on the side of his people. It may not always seem like it, but over and over again, we're told it's true, and we have to trust him in that too. Things may seem dark and dusty, but God will come through, at least on the last day. He says sticking with him is worth it because he sticks with us. Hear his words:

> *The path of the righteous is level; you make level the way of the righteous. In the path of your judgments, O Lord, we wait for you; your name and remembrance are the desire of our soul. My soul yearns for you in the night; my spirit within me earnestly seeks you. For when your judgments are in the earth, the inhabitants of the world learn righteousness.* (Isa. 26:7–9)

Isaiah tells us to walk with God in his path. We walk in his judgments. We wait for him. He becomes our desire, and we earnestly seek him. That's how we learn what is good and righteous.

We're not offering up our righteousness to God. We're not looking around in our hearts and trying to give him the gifts we think he'll take.

It's his city of God he's setting up with his walls and gates. We're looking to him and his ways. We're following his path and his steps. We discern what he thinks is good, and we do those things. We figure out what he thinks is wrong, and we don't do those things. We grieve when we get them mixed up, just like he does. We bring ourselves in this humble position and we spend our lives figuring it out in his love, mercy and grace. This is what sanctification looks like as God slays the dragons in our world and in our lives.

We're not stoics, ignoring the realities of life in this world, in this flesh and blood. We're interested and engaged, and we grieve.

And yet, we're not undone by everything either. We can have a quiet confidence that the Lord is at work, whatever the news report says, whatever we find when we get home, and whatever sleeping on this side of the bed looks like tonight.

God is with us. Our souls yearn for him. Our spirits seek him earnestly, honestly.

We're all familiar with the phrase Rest in Peace or RIP. Rest in Peace can be a trivial way to say something important when someone dies. We carve it on tombstones, hear it at funerals, and see it all over the internet when someone dies. People who were never interested in God get pretty religious at times like this.

I was reading about the phrase Rest in Peace and came across a USA Today article about RIP t-shirts. Religion professor Gary Laderman writes about the history of death, and he says RIP shirts are a growing trend. He writes:

> It used to be that how we remembered the dead and how we understood memorials was much more limited to either a funeral, cemeteries or religious institutions, and in the recent decades its broken out of those areas and has become very much a business. It is part of consumer culture. It is part of how we let people sort of stylize their own experiences of grief. You see it in the rest in peace shirts, body tattoos, decals on the cars and on social media.[6]

So Tim Flowers, the owner of Mall of Memories, will print any type of RIP t-shirt you want. The same article quotes him as saying:

> In pop culture, sometimes the greatest tribute that you can pay to an individual is to wear an article of clothing with them on it. Well, this is the exact same kind of concept in a memorial type of vehicle. What we are finding is this is how modern-age people are mourning now with the T-shirts that some wear to funerals and long after.[7]

Flowers is right. And people want something that will last. A t-shirt seems like it might do the trick. We want to remember. We want peace.

Rest in Peace is a short prayer. God says there will be no rest for the wicked. However, for those who are found in Christ, for those who live out this life we're talking about in Isaiah 26—walking with God, trusting him, waiting for him, none of it done perfectly but earnestly—we will rest in peace forever. Our sorrow is mixed with a great hope in what will happen, that which Jesus himself displayed in his resurrection. Our bodies and souls will be reunited in the new heavens and earth. Every tear will be wiped away, and we'll experience perfect peace forever. There is now no condemnation for those who are in Christ Jesus (Rom. 8:1).

So what about this perfect peace? From our study in Isaiah, we know there would be one who would come as the Prince of Peace (Isa. 9:6).

When Jesus was born, the shepherds heard the angels proclaim *"Glory to God in the highest, and on earth peace among those with whom he is pleased!"* (Luke 2:14).

Jesus said, *"Blessed are the peacemakers, for they shall be called sons of God"* (Matt. 5:9).

Jesus rebuked the wind and the waves in the midst of a great storm, saying, *"Peace! Be still"* (Mark 4:39). And it was so.

Jesus healed in peace. When the bleeding woman touched him, she was afraid, and she trembled. But he turned and looked at her and said, *"'Daughter, your faith has made you well; go in peace, and be healed of your disease'"* (Mark 5:34).

Jesus assured his disciples peace was possible when he said, *"'Peace I leave with you; my peace I give to you. Not as the world gives do I give to you. Let not your hearts be troubled, neither let them be afraid'"* (John 14:27).

When Jesus entered Jerusalem for the Passover, the crowds spread palm branches in his path and yelled, *"'Blessed is the King who comes in the name of the Lord! Peace in heaven and glory in the highest!'"* (Luke 19:38).

When Jesus appeared to his disciples after his resurrection, he said, *"'Peace be with you!'"* (Luke 24:36).

Jesus did say something else. It's true God is a God of love. But he's also just and holy. He punishes sin. He will not let injustice go. And the wages of sin is death. So while Jesus is all about perfect peace, and the flourishing of all things, there will be a judgment. Satan will not flourish. Demons will not get peace. Sin will be done away with, and all who remain in sin and not in Christ. He said, *"Do you think that I have come to give peace on earth? No, I tell you, but rather division"* (Luke 12:50).

It's a sobering reminder in the midst of such encouragement with the Prince of Peace. Peace is—peace for some and a death for others.

Judgment is good for the righteous, but it's painful for the wicked. There is and will be a judgment day, and if you're in the tears business, you'll be sad, not happy.

The Prince of Peace, the Bringer of Shalom, the Divider of All the Wicked did not live his life out in peace. He didn't die an old man retired off on his country estate with a pipe and a rocking chair, his grandkids gathered around. He died a violent death, one of the worst types. This Prince of Peace, Wonderful Counselor, and Mighty God was also the Suffering Servant. He cried out underneath the wrath of God. Like I said, someone has to pay for sins, and the penalty is death. Evil isn't allowed to enter into God's presence. So what's the point and reason God's son died such a death like this?

Jesus took what we deserved. He gave what we didn't earn. He lived for us, and he died for us. So he can bring peace to you and God, to you and me.

It's his righteousness in play here. It's his faithfulness and his steps. His ways make him the way, the truth, and the life.

Jesus doesn't promise nothing bad will ever happen again in this life. That's not the peace he's talking about.

So how can we find it in the midst of our crazy lives?

I haven't talked about greatness yet, and that's been a theme in our thinking about Isaiah.

Mary-Claire heard him say, "Emily and I will be fine."[8] She was so glad to hear someone cared and would help. She certainly didn't expect it to be from this person.

A few days before she heard the man say that, Mary-Claire King's husband told her he was leaving her in April 1981. He'd fallen in love with one of his grad students. This news came as a complete shock to her, and she was devastated. That next day she dropped her five-year-old daughter Emily off at kindergarten, went and taught her college classes, and then she was called into the office by the department head and told she'd gotten tenure. She burst into tears, but pulled herself together, and went and picked up her daughter from school. When they got home, the house was in utter chaos. They'd been robbed that day.

Can you imagine? This is so far from any approximation of peace.

In the midst of all that, Mary-Claire had planned to fly to Washington, DC, to make a presentation. Her daughter was supposed to stay with her husband, but he'd left the picture to go to Costa Rica with his lover. Her mom was going to come to Berkeley to help out, but now Mary-Claire had a whole new situation on her hands with her mom and her daughter.

When Mary-Claire's mom flew in, Mary-Claire told her what had happened, and her mother was upset. She said, "I can't believe you've let this family come apart. I can't believe this child will grow up without a father. How could you do this? How could you not put your family first?" Emily was in the car. After only a few hours, Mary-Claire's mom announced she couldn't take it and wanted to fly back home. Mary-Claire said she'd change the ticket and drop her off at the airport the next day.

So now what?

She called her mentor, and he told her to bring Emily along on the Washington, DC, trip. So they rearranged the flights to make it work.

The next day, the three of them were at the San Francisco airport, but nothing went as planned. Traffic backed up, and they got to the airport late, and their two schedules were off. Her mom was having a tough time with her bags, and Mary-Claire wanted her mom to make it to the plane on her own. She said she couldn't make it. But Mary-Claire couldn't leave Emily.

That's when the man behind her in line said, "Emily and I will be fine." Mary-Claire turned around and said thank you.

Her mom was aghast and shrieked, "You can't leave Emily with a total stranger."

Mary-Claire answered, "Mom, if you can't trust Joe DiMaggio, who can you trust?"

Joe DiMaggio held out his hand and said, "Hi, Emily. I'm Joe." And Emily shook his hand, and said, "Hello Joe. I'm Emily."

Mary-Claire dropped her mom off, and returned and thanked Joe. He said, "My pleasure," with a big grin on his face, gave her a huge salute, and went off to his plane. Mary-Claire and Emily made it to DC, and the presentation went well, and she got a grant that started her work on inherited breast cancer.

———

In the midst of chaos, we can find some peace. We can find a person who can help. We can find the smile of God. We can find a tiny bit of rest. We can find a familiar face who will stand with us when someone else is making it more crazy.

We can trust in someone even greater than Joe DiMaggio showing up at the airport in a crisis. Isaiah tells us:

You keep him in perfect peace whose mind is stayed on you, because he trusts in you. Trust in the Lord forever, for the Lord God is an everlasting rock (Isa. 26:3)

We can rest in peace if he died for us. His dying is our victory. So when we die and our lives end, we can be with him in that victory.

Along the way, we can rest in peace by dying little deaths every day, and experiencing a resurrected life even now. We can die to our impatience, insensibility, doubtfulness, cynicism, biting tongues, gossip, laziness, anger, shutting others out, sarcasm, addictions, annoyances, pet peeves—our sin. And we can hope we'll live all the more in Jesus' peace.

We center on him, til death do us part.

ISAIAH 36–38

Greatness is Jack Bauer in 24.

We (the Servens) re-watched this recently because our kids were too young to see it the first time (and Anna says she cannot stand Jack Bauer!).

You are in the presence of greatness when you are hanging around Jack Bauer. He may seem like a loser sometimes, but he could kill you or save you at any moment. He's the Chuck Norris of our day.

Trust is one of the themes of the show. Nearly every episode someone turns to the other person and says, "You're going to have to trust me on this." Or another variation on this is: "I'll be there. I'll never leave you." When we hear someone say this, we've learned to roll our eyes because we know that seals the deal. The person most certainly will not be there.

"Trust me. I'll be there."

That's what God had told Israel through the prophet Isaiah. Should we roll our eyes when we hear this in the Bible? Through the twists and turns of history and through the mouth and actions of King Ahaz, Israel had done the opposite of trusting God. It had trusted in the nations around her for salvation. It had made alliances with their kings and their gods, and it had forsaken the only one who could truly help it.

But God had not forgotten.

Jack Bauer never forgets. You can count on him.

God is better than Jack Bauer.

Isaiah 36–39 is the climax of the first half of the book. In fact, it is one of the most important events in the Old Testament, validated by the unprecedented three tellings in different passages (our text in Isaiah, and then also in 2 Kings 19ff and 2 Chronicles 32ff). For over a dozen chapters, Isaiah has been recounting the various nations around Israel, how none of them will prevail, and how each of them is ultimately subservient to Yahweh. It's been a geography/sociology/political policy/theology lesson. But now, it's time to put knowledge to action. What will Hezekiah do when faced with destruction?

Let's look at how Hezekiah got to this point and then see what happens.

Hezekiah's Sickness—Prayer One

We turn first to chapter 38. The opening words of the chapter put the timeline into some fuzziness: *"In those days."* We can reconstruct the calendar to determine this chapter's event takes place before what occurs in chapters 36 and 37. Isaiah tells this part later after 36 and 37, but it really happens before those two chapters' events.

Isaiah comes to Hezekiah with these words: *"Thus says the LORD: Set your house in order, for you shall die, you shall not recover"* (Isa. 38:1).

When was the last time you were really, really sick? It's terrible, isn't it? At our last church picnic, twenty to thirty members of our church got food poisoning from the barbecue. That was nasty.

But having the flu is really nothing compared to what some of us go through. I remember visiting one of my RUF students in the hospital for food poisoning. No big deal, right?

He had the worst type you could get, and he almost died. I went to the hospital for another student who had an emergency appendectomy. The next week he was back in the hospital with viral meningitis. Yikes. I have a friend who is 27 and married and had his first child in November. He found out a few months later, in January, he has a serious aggressive cancer.

I hate sickness and death. Here is Hezekiah with the prophet of God in his bedroom, telling him the bad news. He's going to die. We all dread hearing the doctor give the grim diagnosis and the resulting timeframe.

Hezekiah is faced with this intense personal crisis. Our health determines so much about our life. Someday, we will be face to face with our mortality, and I wonder how we will react, especially if it feels as if we are dying before it's our time.

Hezekiah wasn't ready to die. He was thirty-nine years old. In his estimation, he hadn't lived a full life yet, and he also hadn't produced an heir to the throne. (Manasseh came three years after this). By any estimation for a Hebrew man, being cut off childless in midlife was severe judgment from God.

What did Hezekiah do? Did he plunge into a deep depression or think about taking his own life? Did he go on a last hurrah wild trip or try out cryogenics?

He turned to God. We read:

> Then Hezekiah turned his face to the wall and prayed to the LORD, and said, "Please, O LORD, remember how I have walked before you in faithfulness and with a whole heart, and have done what is good in your sight." And Hezekiah wept bitterly. (Isa. 38:2–3)

Faced with death, Hezekiah went to the Lord in prayer. I'm thinking of Johnny Cash's song "Spiritual" where he sings "Jesus, Jesus, I don't want to die alone. Jesus if you hear my last prayer, don't leave me here alone to die my last breath."

Hezekiah's prayer isn't a great one. It was short, weak, and general. Hezekiah hadn't done everything right, but he had been faithful to God. It was a true prayer from the heart.

Not all our prayers have to be amazing works of art. One of my favorite prayer books is one written by the Puritans called, *The Valley of Vision*. I'm encouraged and challenged by this collection of prayers and the topics they cover. They're astounding.

But they're not my normal prayers, and they probably weren't theirs either. They took time to write them, but I'm sure they had spontaneous short prayers all the time in normal, everyday life. We don't have to cram everything in our prayers and have perfect theology all the time. Prayer is talking with God, and sometimes we can shoot a conversation up there that says, "Help," or "I need you," or "Save me," or "Really?!," or "I hate this," or "Thank you!" Anne Lamott has a book where she says her most often and most profound prayers are "Help," "Thanks," and "Wow."

God answered Hezekiah's short prayer. God sent Isaiah back to Hezekiah with a different message. This time he said:

> Thus says the LORD, the God of David your father: I have heard your prayer; I
> have seen your tears. Behold, I will add fifteen years to your life. I will deliver
> you and this city out of the hand of the king of Assyria, and will defend this city.
> (Isa. 38:4–6)

God shows his faithfulness to Hezekiah by listening and answering his prayer. He mentions the covenant with David as an indication of his commitments in the past. Unlike the idols of wood and stone that surround Jerusalem, Yahweh hears and sees. He is moved by his people. God knows and intervenes in the lives of his people. Hezekiah had fifteen more years which is pretty good.

God doesn't always respond to a prayer like this with a "Yes" answer. Sometimes, many times even, he says "No." Or "Not yet." Or "Maybe." Or even "I'm not telling you." But sometimes he does answer with a "Yes," and he did this time.

Not only that, but Hezekiah asked for and is given a sign to assure him of God's trustworthiness. His faith was weak, but he was disposed to believe. This is in contrast to Ahaz, who had refused to accept a sign when one was offered in chapter 7. This is the difference between light and darkness, between faith and unbelief. It may not be strong faith all the time, but it is trust and belief.

The sign was awesome. God sent the sun backward (Isa. 38:7–8). You can imagine a weak and sickly Hezekiah looking out his window at the sundial in the courtyard. He wants to believe in his healing, but really it is difficult to see such a miracle taking place. And then, the sun moves backward, and he knows God is faithful. When God says, "Trust me," he means it. Hezekiah had asked for a sign and gotten it.

It's interesting to note that the way the recovery happened was mundane. No big production involved. In Isaiah 38:21, we read,

"Now Isaiah had said, 'Let them take a cake of figs and apply it to the boil, that he may recover.'" God can show his power both in the receding sun and in a bandaid on the boil.

Hezekiah's Kingship—Prayer Two

Hezekiah survives, and he later has a son. He continues his program of reformation. All is well. Except.... We go back to Isaiah 36:1 and read: *"In the fourteenth year of King Hezekiah, Sennacherib king of Assyria came up against all the fortified cities of Judah and took them."*

All around him, the nations are falling to Sennacherib. People Hezekiah knew, his colleagues—the kings of Hamath, Arpad, Sepharvaim, Hena, and of Ivvah—were wiped out by this Assyrian king.

We have good records of the historicity of all this. Sennacherib had his conquests written down and reliefs made of his victories. One of them was about when he conquered the city of Lachish. It can be seen in the British Museum in London. This stuff really happened. It's substantiated.

And now, on the doorstep of Jerusalem, this general has Hezekiah trapped "like a caged bird." Sennacherib's emissary Rabshekah stands at the gates and gives a brutal, taunting speech calling Yahweh's people's policies and theology in question. All of what he says has truth sprinkled into it.

Much, if not most, of what he says is true. The nations, cities, and the kings around Jerusalem all had gods too. They all prayed and trusted too. And they have all been carted off, enslaved, and destroyed. Why would Israel think its god would be any different? In fact, these nations were stronger than this little dinky city—they should be more afraid, not more confident. Soon they will be eating dung and drinking urine.

Gross. Humiliating. Overwhelming.

The gauntlet has been thrown down.

God's people hear someone say God is not the sovereign. The flash prophet is crying out:

> Righteousness will not prevail. It is the nations of man with whom all must come to terms. God, whoever you are—if you are—human might

and human glory will dictate to you the limits of your action or being. Your God sucks. Your God is no good. Your God is impotent. Your God is fooling you. You God is weak. Your God will fail you. Your God is all talk and no action, just like everyone else. Your God is an illusion. Your God is an imagination, a construction of what you wish to be true. Why would you trust in that? Wake up!

Does this sound familiar at all? It seems so modern. We have prophets who state this very thing in our world today. They cry out:

If you believe in God you're weak or crazy or immature or stupid or backward. Trust in science! Trust in yourself! Trust in the zodiac and astrology! Trust in the goodness of mankind! Trust in upward advancement! Trust your feelings!

What will we do? Whom shall we believe and follow? Who are our prophets? We all believe something is ultimate. We all have a bottom line. What's yours?

The logic is that God's people should surrender because this man —this king, general, and ruler Sennacherib—is stronger than God (who may be made up anyway). We rarely are presented with such a blunt decision, and yet we are faced with this every day.

We're tempted to think God either cannot or will not help us, so we must rely on human strength.

We do this with our bodies, studies, careers, affections, finances, alliances, minds, and our opinions

We say, "God's way? Ha."

We think:

If God exists—a big if—then he cannot help me here. Not in my singleness. Not as a single mom, a divorced dad, or as a widow. Not in my same sex attraction. Not in my marriage. Not with my parents or my failing friendships. Not with my grievances. Not with my past and family background. Not with my debt. Not as a foreigner or as a refugee. Not with this skin color. Not with this disability.

If God does exist at all, don't you know he helps those who help themselves? If God exists, he doesn't care about little problems like this one. If God exists, he just doesn't understand what I'm going through. He cannot help me. He doesn't care. He isn't there at all.

Do you ever feel this way? I sure do sometimes. I don't believe God is there or can help, even when I have been afforded every privilege possible. I have all this, and I still doubt God's presence and goodness. Hezekiah must have felt that way too. He was faced with tremendous evidence to bolster just this idea.

He's a Jewish man in his late thirties who is dying without children, and his very people are about to be attacked by the most powerful army in the world. He's about to be wiped out, and everything he cares about will be too. All will be destroyed.

Perhaps this is a good time to doubt God. It seems fairly reasonable.

I was watching *Wonder Woman* recently. The movie takes place during World War I, and there's a scene where a whole town is wiped out by the Germans. If you watch war movies, you're familiar with this. Everyone has been killed. Everything is destroyed. There's nothing and no one left except remnants of life. King Hezekiah was about to face that type of annihilation.

We can hardly imagine what it would have been like to be wiped out like this.

After the 2013 EF5 tornado in Moore, I drove down to ground zero the day afterward. I was allowed in through the barricades because I was wearing my pastor's collar.

No one was around. As the rain fell, the silence was amazing. No cars, people., or activity. Houses lay in ruin block after block after block.

What if it were like that because the whole city had been bombed, and it was city after city, and people were dead on the streets and walking with carts, starving and trying to escape with whatever they could carry? Would you trust in God then? In the concentration camps? In the cramped, crowded refugee villages where people spend an average of twenty years?

And don't we feel like that's a picture of what's going on in our own hearts? Bombs have gone off in our personal lives, with our finances, with our loneliness, with who has touched us and whom we have touched, with things said to us, and things we've said.

There is death in our lives. Sadness and darkness that we may never forget. We're a wounded, scarred people.

When you feel like that, you may doubt. I would. Seems reasonable, normal, and understandable.

But the Bible shows us we should do just what Hezekiah did. Hezekiah sent for Isaiah. He needed a word from the Lord! He needed some guidance, counseling, and hope.

You can send for Isaiah too. You can turn to him in your Bibles in times of crisis and read what he said, which was this: "Nothing else can be trusted, but God can be."

Somehow, by the work of the Holy Spirit in the lives of these sinners and saints, in the midst of crisis, "Judah lurched awake" and realized Isaiah's words were really true. This realization brought about the reaction of repentance. Hezekiah went to the Lord's house to admit his nation's folly and its foolish dependence on Egypt. There was an admission of helplessness, failure, and fear. But also a hope for things going forward. The weak mother still must bear the child. You can't put it off. It has to happen. There is no turning back. Help is needed, but help can be gotten.

So Hezekiah does what he had learned to do when he was sick. He prayed.

This time it goes this way:

> O LORD of hosts, God of Israel, who is enthroned above the cherubim, you are the God, you alone, of all the kingdoms of the earth; you have made heaven and earth. Incline your ear, O LORD, and hear; open your eyes, O LORD, and see; and hear all the words of Sennacherib, which he has sent to mock the living God. Truly, O LORD, the kings of Assyria have laid waste all the nations and their lands, and have cast their gods into the fire. For they were no gods, but the work of men's hands, wood and stone. Therefore they were destroyed. So now, O LORD our God, save us from his hand, that all the kingdoms of the earth may know that you alone are the LORD. (Isa. 37:16–20)

This is a great prayer! Hezekiah has learned about the faithfulness and trustworthiness of God. Perhaps he got a preview copy of the

Valley of Visions prayer book. He knows God can come through, so he goes to him for help.

Why? What is his basis for asking? Hezekiah's greatest concern is for the honor of God.

As you look at Hezekiah's prayer, you see he talks about God, about the Lord. He recounts God's glory, holiness, transcendence, and awesomeness.

That is something Sennacherib and Rabshekah hadn't counted on. What if Yahweh wasn't bound by this world, but he created it? That would be different than the other gods, wouldn't it?

Hezekiah is also specific. He mentions Sennacherib and the situation he's in. He asks God to save them so that all the kingdoms of the earth might know he alone is God. This is the God Isaiah has been talking about. Will he answer? Can he be trusted? Will he come through? What will happen?

God tells Hezekiah, "Trust me."

Through Isaiah, God says, "Sennacherib is my enemy. He is too far gone to change. I will show him my wrath and judgment. He is like an animal with a bridle, and I the Lord turn him wherever I wish. Do not worry. A remnant will always remain."

"Trust me." Ah, but can we?

What happens next is surprising in its stark, fact-reporting style. The hard work has been done. Now it is merely to be brought about. Isaiah writes:

> And the angel of the LORD went out and struck down a hundred and eighty-five thousand in the camp of the Assyrians. And when people arose early in the morning, behold, these were all dead bodies. Then Sennacherib king of Assyria departed and returned home and lived at Nineveh. And as he was worshiping in the house of Nisroch his god, Adrammelech and Sharezer, his sons, struck him down with the sword. And after they escaped into the land of Ararat, Esarhaddon his son reigned in his place. (Isa. 37:36–38)

God saved Jerusalem through a great deliverance, and God's people were rescued!

Sennacherib went home. In his own accounts, he doesn't mention why he left Jerusalem standing, but he never claims to have conquered it. Years later, his sons murdered him in the temple of his god just like he had wanted to kill Hezekiah.

God saved his people. God answers prayer. God is faithful. God is trustworthy. God is mighty to save. God sees. God hears. God knows. God intervenes. God is like no one else.

We may cringe at the way God did it, but this is like when the Allied Forces went in and saved the cities where the concentration camps were built. We destroyed destroyers. God delivered his people with this miracle. It's why we're here today talking about this.

Can you pray like Hezekiah here? Can you talk to God in your desperate need? What has been your most earnest prayer?

Where do you need rescue in your life? Where do others need rescue, and can you pray for God to come through for them too?

Do you believe this?

Hezekiah's Legacy—A Psalm

Hezekiah is now counted as one of Judah's great kings. He is greatly esteemed and rightly so.

This event saved Jerusalem. When we look back to chapter 38 and how God saved Hezekiah from his illness, we see his psalm of praise. And we know what has already happened in the saving of Jerusalem because of the odd configuration of the time elements of these two narratives. The miraculous healing occurred before the miraculous redemption in time but after in the telling of the story.

Everything is done, and Hezekiah reflects on what the experience has meant to him.

Hezekiah learns a tough lesson, and he responds:

God never left me. He was there all along. And that means he gave this burden to me, for whatever reason. He's not the author of sin. That cannot be. But he is not gone. He overwhelms and superintends in a way I cannot understand. This story is my story he meant me to have, whatever this sickness is for me, whatever has happened in my life. He loves me. He is with me. That always has been and will always be true, thy kingdom come thy will be done on earth as it is in heaven.

Hezekiah is alive, and Jerusalem is safe.

But not forever.

Hezekiah is going to die. This good and righteous king is not the Messiah, not the final, ultimate true one. And Hezekiah leaves behind someone who plunges Judah into disaster. Manasseh is one of the worst kings, undoing all his father's reforms.

Hezekiah seems to sow the seeds of his own demise. He lets in the envoys of Babylon, making a pact too easily and too quickly with them as shown in chapter 39. Isaiah 39 foreshadows this fall. Isaiah knew that in the long-term, Babylon would prove to be an enemy rather than a friend.

This deliverance story in the book of Isaiah about the history of our chosen people is not one that describes heaven. Hezekiah is not the King of Kings and Lord of Lords in his final day and final glory.

The new heavens and new earth are yet to come. The Messiah still has not arrived.

In the midst of that realization, in the midst of real life, and yet with pictures of redemption and pictures of the messiah, Hezekiah reflected this way:

I said, In the middle of my days I must depart; I am consigned to the gates of Sheol for the rest of my years. I said, I shall not see the LORD, the LORD in the land of the living; I shall look on man no more among the inhabitants of the world. My dwelling is plucked up and removed from me like a shepherd's tent; like a weaver I have rolled up my life; he cuts me off from the loom; from day to night you bring me to an end; I calmed myself until morning; like a lion he breaks all my bones; from day to night you bring me to an end. Like a swallow or a crane I chirp; I moan like a dove. My eyes are weary with looking upward. O Lord, I am oppressed; be my pledge of safety! What shall I say? For he has spoken to me, and he himself has done it. I walk slowly all my years because of the bitterness of my soul. O Lord, by these things men live, and in all these is the life of my spirit. Oh restore me to health and make me live! Behold, it was for my welfare that I had great bitterness; but in love you have delivered my life from the pit of destruction, for you have cast all my sins behind your back. For Sheol does not thank you; death does not praise you; those who go down to the pit do not hope for your faithfulness. The living, the living, he thanks you, as I do this day; the father makes known to the children your faithfulness. The LORD will save me,

and we will play my music on stringed instruments all the days of our lives, at
the house of the LORD. (Isa. 38:10–20)

God disciplines those whom he loves, for our good and his glory. We need to call out to him to save us, no matter what that means. My friend Josh Spears tells a story about his son when he was a young boy. Aiden got in trouble in front of a group of people, and as Josh took him to get disciplined, Aiden turned to the group and yelled to them, "Help!"

He needed to ask his father for help, but he asked the group instead. He was appealing to the wrong authorities. Josh still disciplined him, and he did so to save Aiden from the greater danger of his sin. Sin leads to death, and it's better to be shown that pain earlier rather than later. When Josh disciplined Aiden, he brought pain into Aiden's life to save him from a deeper, longer pain. Aiden's help came, but not as he had expected. Josh was a good father.

On your blog, in your journal, in your thoughts and prayers, could you say:

Behold, it was for my welfare that I had great bitterness; but in love you have
delivered my life from the pit of destruction, for you have cast all my sins behind
your back. For Sheol does not thank you; death does not praise you; those who go
down to the pit do not hope for your faithfulness. The living, the living, he
thanks you, as I do this day; the father makes known to the children your
faithfulness. The LORD will save me, and we will play my music on stringed
instruments all the days of our lives, at the house of the LORD. (Isa. 39:17–20)

God saved his people for his sake. They were not perfect nor righteous. He did not have to rescue them.

But he did, and it was not an idea or a theorem outside of reality. It happened in real time and space. He did so for his glory.

Death and life are before you. Oppression and bitterness are all around you. Evil. Hatred. Pride. Self-sufficiency.

The world and its powers have a good case. They have evidence. Believing in God seems like foolishness. The church is a whore to be sure. Hurt is at every corner. Injustice seems to prevail, and the bad guys too often win.

The message of Christianity says life and peace can be had, but only by faith. There are certainly signs, but they must be trusted and believed in. There is forgiveness from the father who loves his children. There is salvation in a Redeemer of God's elect.

At the 45th Presbyterian Church in America's (PCA) General Assembly in Greensboro, North Carolina, I was the chairman of the Administrative Committee of Commissioners. I was trying to be more involved instead of staying behind the scenes and just complaining like I had previously. So whereas before I'd go and hang out, meet people, have coffee and drinks, and see my friends, that year I spent time preparing, reading the docket and reports, discussing things, sitting in the room for all the reports, voting, and even speaking on the floor. I would have never in a million years guessed I'd ever be doing that. We had to present our report and our thirty one recommendations before the assembly at 10:45 p.m. on Thursday.

It was a beat down, and I would hit my hotel room exhausted. I think there is a ring in Dante's inferno reserved for hours of debate on the minutiae of Robert's Rules of Order. To be sure, it was fun to stay up late with friends, meet new ones, and talk about weird things that cannot seem to matter. I'm guessing the Uber drivers have never overheard conversations like the ones we'd have on our way to eat or go places—about the regulative principle, the Review of Presbytery Records Minority Report on the breaking of the second commandment, on budgets and overture number two being sent back to the committee for next year, on the stated clerk's opinion on the formation of a new presbytery.... I can't believe I'm even writing about this now!

On Thursday of that week, I sat in the same room with about a thousand pastors and elders for about ten hours. I nearly went insane.

In the midst of all that chaos in the room and in my own heart, I was glad to do the business of the church. I love the church, and I was glad to argue, debate, win votes and lose votes.

Isaiah writes: *"Let them take a cake of figs and apply it to the boil, that he may recover'"* (Isa. 38:21). I needed some fig cakes on my boils for sure.

Those were applied, and I was especially glad when we worshiped. My friend Joel Littlepage put together some of the greatest worship services I have ever been to. The music was incredible. We sang in Korean and Spanish. The arrangements of the songs were some of the best I'd ever heard. I heard my friends George, Irwyn, and Duke preach the Word of God. I was convicted, and I wept at the grace and goodness of God for sinners like me. I was able to sit in deep fellowship with my brothers and the few sisters who were there. We laughed, cried for each other, worked out, discussed, and caught up. I felt healed for a time.

There were redemptive moments in the midst of the difficulty. It wasn't heaven. Please Lord, let heaven not follow Robert's Rules! But the Redeemer was there. God was with us.

Hezekiah died fifteen years later. He was spared for a time, but he died soon enough. It makes me think of Lazarus, whom Jesus raised from the dead. Wouldn't that have been amazing to see? Absolutely phenomenal. Yet, Lazarus died later. Who knows how much longer he lived. The stories he could have told. But he died again.

And Jerusalem fell. It wasn't ultimately saved after all. It was for a time, but later it was taken over. The stories the people could have told about Sennarcherib's army falling before them! What fireside chats those would have made. But then, such disappointment when all came to ruin again, the city ransacked, and the temple destroyed.

Maybe being protected from those things isn't the point after all. God might send us these situations, deaths, pains, and sicknesses in order that we would see our desperate need for him, cry out to him, and see him for who he is—the Savior of our souls, the Redeemer. The one who conquered death by taking it so we could live. The one who was ransacked so we could be restored. The one who took the full weight of all God's wrath, so we could stand before him as his sons and his daughters.

What happened in these chapters in Isaiah were miracles, redemptive ones that pointed to the work of God on behalf of his people to save them. But these only pointers to the true redemptive miracle: he sent his son to live and die for his people, for his children.

Do you see that sign? Do you believe Jesus came to seek and to save the lost and that he is the True Rescuer? That he might even overwhelm and redeem the sadness and wrong things in your life? That he especially loves the injured, downcast, poor in spirit, mourners, marginalized, and weak?

Those are all things we especially hate to be, and yet those are the very ones in whom the Lord loves the most.

We read in John 5:24:

Truly, truly, I say to you, whoever hears my word and believes him who sent me has eternal life. He does not come into judgment, but has passed from death to life.

We serve a God who rescues. He did then in a big way, and he still does now. We long for and look for it. And we need to talk about it. Remember the end of Hezekiah's middle prayer? We read him say, *"So now, O LORD our God, save us from his hand, that all the kingdoms of the earth may know that you alone are the LORD"* (Isa. 37:20).

So that all the kingdoms of the earth may know you alone are the Lord. When we tell our stories the world knows just a little bit better about our rescuing God.

Are you ready to tell your story? It's really a Hezekiah tale, albeit not nearly as dramatic. And it's really a story about the Deliverer, not about you. It's all about Jesus.

This true Isaiah history only points to the full story of the real, full Savior Jesus Christ—our prophet, priest, and king. Follow him. Give yourself to him. Trust in him. Believe him.

He's better than Jack Bauer, far better. Trust him with your story too.

ISAIAH 40

We're thinking about what it means to be in the presence of greatness. I (Doug) recently asked people, "What was something you used to think was awesome and amazing, but later found out there was something way, way better?" I received some pretty good answers: my Palm Pilot, Gateway 2000 computers, the Backstreet Boys, xanga, JNCO jeans, 90s Christian praise and worship music, The Left Behind series, 9am classes your freshman year (now it's 1:30pm classes), Creed, Coors Light, margarine, Miracle Whip, Mountain Dew, Funyuns, Garfield, former girlfriends, and tricycles....

For a good perspective on what used to be awesome, watch Steve Jobs introduce the first Macintosh computer in 1984.[1]

Things change. Anything can seem pretty great, but it can fade over time. It's rare if you appreciate an item more and more the longer you have it. Most objects wear out quickly, or your fascination fades, or you move on to something better. No one has a 1G iPhone anymore.

Which makes you wonder—what will last? What do you love that will soon be replaced? Who is singing "It's Friday" anymore?

We need to reset ourselves in the book of Isaiah. We're trying to understand each passage of Isaiah we come to, but we also need to be able to see Isaiah as a whole.

Chapter 40 begins a new section of the book. Isaiah looks forward in his prophetic crystal ball. God allows Isaiah to see forward, and Isaiah sees captivity for his people but also deliverance.

Isaiah has just told his people that they would be carried off by Babylon. At the end of chapter 39, Isaiah would have been sixty-nine years old. By the time Hezekiah dies three years later, Isaiah would have been seventy two. Tradition says he died as a martyr during the reign of Manasseh, who had him sawn in two. Isaiah had been preaching to the people of his day about the nations around them and how they would come to ruin at the hand of God. Now Isaiah is preaching to a future people in Babylonian captivity, which began years later in 586 BC.

As an aside, this passage is where most scholars began espousing the "Second Isaiah" theory (for this reason—peering ahead into the future is considered impossible). Its tone and content is assuredly different from the previous chapters, so they posit there must be a different, later author. Critical theory then supposed a "Third Isaiah," and we might imagine there could be even more.

How can we answer this, considering Jesus himself quoted from this section of the book and attributed it to Isaiah? Isaiah 1–39 is written to a people facing the Assyrians in the eighth century, and the rest of the book to the exiles in Babylon in the sixth century BC.

It might be possible for me to write a letter to my daughter in the future, one she's meant to open when she is twenty five or thirty five. If I know her well, I might be able to project forward and talk to her in a real way, assuring her of many things in the midst of her struggles. If so, why wouldn't we believe in the mini-miracle of the ability, brought about by God, of this part of the book? An implication of this could be—if we cannot believe in such a mini-miracle, then why would we believe in the major miracle of the resurrection? If you take the improbable out of life, you don't have anything that requires faith.

Let's take Isaiah on his own terms, and let's believe God can speak through his prophets.

In *The Hitchhiker's Guide to the Galaxy,* by Douglas Adams, philosophers asked the computer Deep Thought what was the answer to Life, The Universe and Everything.

The answer took 7.5 million years to come up with. And the answer was… forty two.

Now they had the answer, so all they needed was the question.

Let's ask some questions.

Who Is Able to Save Us?

We have a people in exile. Here in the US, we cannot imagine what that is like. Picture the Jewish people bombed with air raids so they have to leave their families, houses, and all they know. They were carted off and taken far away. They had nothing. They suffered, were lonely, and they were chastened. They had not listened, had not trusted God, and they had been disciplined by him. Was this the end? Was God giving up on them?

By the mercies of God, we haven't suffered that type of fate. But we do have situations we're caught in, places where we are stuck—exiled as it were. Can you think of anywhere in your life where you need saving? How will you get out of that trap?

Who is able to save us?

The answer is God. Not you. If you could save yourself, you would have already.

We receive a ton of well-meaning, awful advice. Stop eating so much. Exercise more. Have more self-control. Don't do it anymore. Just stop. Stay away from him.

If you could, you would have already.

We need something else, something better. God is able. He tells them so in 40:12–31. God is awesome. He is the only thing that is. That word should be reserved for him alone, for he's the only one who can fill it with meaning.

God is the answer, but he asks some questions himself, ones we need to answer.

Who has measured the waters in the hollow of his hand? How much water can you hold in the palm of your hand? Stick your hand out right now and manipulate it into the configuration you think will get you the most holding ability. How much water can you hold? Three or four tablespoons?

God says he can measure all the waters in his. The total water supply of the world is 326 million cubic miles (a cubic mile is an imaginary cube (a square box) measuring one mile on each side). A cubic mile of water equals more than one trillion gallons. So, if my math is right, then the gallons of water in this world is equal to 326 million times one trillion. Someone figure out how much that is for me. It's a whooooooole lot. That's how big God is.

Who enclosed the dust of the earth in a measure and weighed the mountains in scales and the hills in a balance? As you know, the earth is bigger than just the waters on it. What can I paint as a picture for you to see just how big it is? If a skydiver could fall into an opening in the earth and continue to fall at the same speed—without being destroyed by the intense heat in the earth's core—how long would it take him from the earth's surface to reach the center of the earth? I've been skydiving, and the whole skydiving part lasts about twenty seconds. So how long would it take to reach the center of the earth? It would take forty-two minutes. Our speck is bigger than we think.[2]

But it flirts with insignificance when compared to the universe.

Who marked off the heavens with a span? This is important because the Babylonians were great astrologers; in fact, they worshiped the heavenly bodies. Commentator Ortland writes, "The constellations the Babylonians believed were controlling the destinies of man are themselves controlled by *God*."[3]

To mark off a space with a span is to spread your fingers out and measure from the tip of your thumb to the tip of your little finger. So it's an irregular measurement but within a certain range as long as you exclude pro basketball players. Mine is about six inches.

The nearest star is four and a half light years away. Light travels at 186,000 miles per second. The nearest star is 26 trillion miles away —26,000,000,000,000. That is just the nearest star.

The Milky Way galaxy is an estimated 104,000 light years across and contains over 100 billion stars. To count them one by one would take 3,000 years. There are guessed to be hundreds of billions of galaxies in the universe. Astronomers deal in massively large, incomprehesible numbers. They have to make up other ways to figure and speak of these distances. God says the universe—not even just our galaxy but the whole universe—is something he can mark off with his hand.

The rest of the chapter continues in this theme. You know how when you fly in a plane and look out on a clear day, and you can see towns, rivers and sometimes when you're close enough, the cars? God's perspective is like that all the time.

We're like grasshoppers. We're small and easily squish-able. He's not afraid of us. When Mr. Miyagi calls Daniel a grasshopper in *The Karate Kid*, he's saying he doesn't know anything about the subject at hand.

The greatest figures ever in the world—the pharaohs, the dictators, the presidents, the generals, the philosophers, the writers, the pop stars—they are like nothing. Like dust and grass. They are blowing in the wind. The greatest nations—Assyria, Babylonia, Greece, Rome, Portugal, and Spain ruled the world at one time. Now we have England, China, Russia, and the United States—they are zippo to God. He is outside of time. He sees and encompasses all.

Something made this world. Even if you want to go back to the Big Bang—what caused that? How can something come out of nothing?[4]

Isaiah's sarcasm drips from each line as he describes the "power" of idols. Isaiah laughs at the foolishness of following things made of wood, stone, and gold. You think idols will save you? You think other gods could compare to Yahweh?

Perhaps we could say Isaiah pits professional bodybuilders against the world's strongest man. You can see both of these competitions on ESPN now and then, especially when top-level programming is sparse.

Professional bodybuilders are caricatures of real people. You'll be startled if you look at pictures of them on the internet. They have accentuated proportions, and most people know this is just not natural. Something is wrong. Can we say—steroids? They stand up on stage, pose, strut, and flex, and—what is going on?

But the world's strongest man is just that—strong. The whole competition is based on plausible activities that show strength. Carrying a really heavy rock a really long way. Lifting a huge pole up the steps. Pulling a truck might be useful at some point in your life. These people are strong, and I'm sure they train and lift, but it's a real strength.

If I need someone to flex, I'll call a bodybuilder. If I need someone to lift a truck up because my wife is trapped underneath it, it's the world's strongest man. His strength matters to me in the real world. It's not for show.

God is the universe's strongest man. He is not a caricature. He is not a monster. He is not out of proportion and sterile. He is real and able to help.

We can ask Isaiah's question for our day.

Do you think idols will save you? Do you think other gods could compare to Yahweh?

You fashion a relationship, you cast it with affection, and overlay it with sex. But it will not last. Like a skilled craftsman, you can build a career, but it will fail you. He can blow on it all, and it will wither.

Who is able to save? God is able.

Who Is Willing to Save?

But is God willing? That is a different question.

In his song "Chicago," Sufjan Stevens sings over and over, "I made a lot of mistakes. I made a lot of mistakes."

We can all sing that song. I've made a lot of mistakes in the last twenty-four hours. You have. Israel had. The Bible calls that sin. Isaiah refers to it here as "iniquity." We are sinners at the hands of a mighty God.

Look at all Israel had done to screw up. That's what Isaiah 1–39 is about. There are sins in those first 39 chapters that Democrats like to talk about, but Republicans like to shy away from. Like social justice, fairness, equality, people's rights.

There are sins that Republicans talk about and Democrats don't. Like personal sin, morality, and faith.

Both are wrong. Both have blown it. Concentrating on just one side is a way to get out of dealing with the sins you have in your own life.[5]

If you can't say "I've made a lot of mistakes," then the rest of the book of Isaiah is not for you. You are not listening to God, and you do not understand yourself.

But if you can say you're a sinner, then you need hope. Ortland writes:

> As we see more and more of life, we are confronted with disappointment so persistently and so convincingly, hope starts to look just plain stupid. We become disappointed in our ideals, disappointed in romance, disappointed in our careers, disappointed in the people we trust, disappointed in ourselves. When all human hopes have let us down, we might be ready for the only real salvation that exists.[6]

You may be in exile. You need hope from someone who can provide it to you. That hope comes from God, for he is willing to save, even though your mistakes, sins, and iniquity should disqualify you. Faith is not all struggle. It is also release and new beginnings.

There is resurrection.

Keep in mind the awesome vision of God's mightiness during the rest of the chapter. That Mighty God, that Yahweh, speaks to Isaiah, saying, *"Comfort, comfort my people, says your God"* (Isa. 40:1). God brings comfort.

Do you need comfort? Do you need friends? Do you need someone who loves you and listens to you, someone who knows you?

You also need someone who will be honest with you. Someone who brings some judgment, who knows right from wrong, and who calls you to be better and to trust. In the deepest places where you're afraid to tell people, you need comfort.

God says he will comfort *his people*. Commentator Oswalt writes:

God's trustworthiness does not end at the point of disobedience. He was the Lord of history who delivered those who would obey, and he continues to be the Lord of history to deliver those would disobey but would then turn to him in faith.[7]

He loves his people. He grieves for them, and he comforts them. The comfort has content:

Speak tenderly to Jerusalem, and cry to her that her warfare is ended, that her iniquity is pardoned, that she has received from the Lord's hand double for all her sins. (Isa. 40:2).

The content of the comfort of God is forgiveness. Rejoice in forgiveness. Warfare can be ended. Iniquity is pardoned. In fact, she has received from the Lord's hand double payment for all her sins. What does that mean? It doesn't mean she has to pay twice. It means we're given so much more, set free, and blessed beyond belief.

Many Christians think God's grace is the pardon of their sins. And yes, that is true. It's an amazing grace.

But it's not all there is. For if it were, it feels like a resetting of things. It would be sort of like being released from jail, which would be glorious, but when you go to buy a house or get a job, you find out your reputation is ruined. You cannot function in society. You're excited because you've been pardoned, but you cannot escape your past life. This is common for prisoners, and it's the way we think God must work too when we're set free.

Christians live that way. But God says he gives double for your sins. Like a piece of paper folded in half, it means yes he forgives you for your old life, but he also gives the corresponding new life, one that replaces your identity as far as he's concerned. You are set free in newness. You've received double for your sins. That is good news.

Oswalt puts it this way:

The path to servanthood for Israel lay through an experience of the utterly unmerited grace of God. He was not required to deliver them. They had been amply warned of the consequences of their disbelief. If they persisted, as persist they would, God would have no obligation to them whatsoever. Yet these chapters speak of a god who, knowing his people would forsake him, nevertheless promises in advance to redeem them, and that "without silver and without price."[8]

God is able to do this because he's a king. Isaiah writes:

> *A voice cries: "In the wilderness prepare the way of the LORD; make straight in the desert a highway for our God. Every valley shall be lifted up, and every mountain and hill be made low; the uneven ground shall become level, and the rough places a plain. And the glory of the LORD shall be revealed, and all flesh shall see it together, for the mouth of the LORD has spoken."* (Isa. 40:3–5)

Kings can pardon. And the king is showing up in your town. You don't have to go to London to meet the king and hear his pardon. He's coming to where you live, to the wilderness, outskirts, the hinterlands, to your cul-de-sac. That is the imagery we have here, for when a king was to travel, new satisfactory roads had to be built. This is a king of a different nature. He doesn't build around or through, but he completely changes the topography itself. That's how powerful he is.

In comparison, we are reminded that we are like nothing really. It's the king's word that stands forever.

Grass comes and goes. I can't grow any in my yard, and when it does come, it burns up. But God's Word isn't like grass or flowers. It stands forever. In fact, that is why we're looking at it right now.

Seeing God's comfort and his double pardon. Seeing your life accounted to him and his life accounted to you. When you look at your mistakes and hear God's pardoning words, you can't help but worship him. We read:

> *Get you up to a high mountain, O Zion, herald of good news; lift up your voice with strength, O Jerusalem, herald of good news; lift it up, fear not; say to the cities of Judah, "Behold your God!" Behold, the Lord God comes with might, and his arm rules for him; behold, his reward is with him, and his recompense before him.* (Isa. 40:9–10)

We sing, "Don't hide it under a bushel, NO! This little light of mine, I'm gonna let it shine."

Let it shine. Herald the good news of God's grace. Lift up your voice with strength. Don't be afraid. Say to your friends, your family, your neighborhood, your work: "Behold your God!"

God isn't saving his people with programs from afar. He isn't saving his people with theological concepts coolly administered. He isn't saving his people through social programs designed to increase their wealth. He comes! That's how he saves his people—he comes.

God is a king, and he is coming. Make way. Make straight the path, for he will rule. We need to be his people. Not the campus screamers, but in our conversations and lifestyles, we proclaim God is real, he is living and active, he is involved in our lives, and he reorders and restructures.

So What?

That has to be true. We long for it to be true. Is it true for you?

Look at the passage again. We have the awesome creator God coming to give comfort, forgiveness, and his life for his people. He comes as a king, and he comes, as per verse 11, in meekness as a shepherd:

> He will tend his flock like a shepherd; he will gather the lambs in his arms; he will carry them in his bosom, and gently lead those that are with young. (Isa. 40:11)

Who are we talking about? In the 700s BC, Isaiah prophecies that the future king is coming.

In the first century AD, the four gospel writers all say the king has come:

> In those days John the Baptist came preaching in the wilderness of Judea, "Repent, for the kingdom of heaven is at hand." For this is he who was spoken of by the prophet Isaiah when he said, "The voice of one crying in the wilderness: 'Prepare the way of the Lord; make his paths straight.'" (Matt. 3:1–3)
>
> The beginning of the gospel of Jesus Christ, the Son of God. As it is written

in Isaiah the prophet, "Behold, I send my messenger before your face, who will prepare your way, the voice of one crying in the wilderness: 'Prepare the way of the Lord, make his paths straight'" (Mark 1:1–3)

As it is written in the book of the words of Isaiah the prophet, "The voice of one crying in the wilderness: 'Prepare the way of the Lord, make his paths straight. (Luke 3:4)

Are you the Prophet?" And he answered, "No." So they said to him, "Who are you? We need to give an answer to those who sent us. What do you say about yourself?" He said, "I am the voice of one crying out in the wilderness, 'Make straight the way of the Lord,' as the prophet Isaiah said." (Now they had been sent from the Pharisees.) They asked him, "Then why are you baptizing, if you are neither the Christ, nor Elijah, nor the Prophet?" John answered them, "I baptize with water, but among you stands one you do not know, even he who comes after me, the strap of whose sandal I am not worthy to untie." These things took place in Bethany across the Jordan, where John was baptizing. (John 1:21–28)

All four claim John the Baptist as the one making the way and building the roads for the king Jesus of Nazareth, and they do so by quoting our passage here in Isaiah 40.

Jesus is the Creator, Warrior, and the Shepherd King who saves sinners and brings them comfort. The creator of the world has come all the way down into the womb of Mary to be born in a stable, to live in poverty and obscurity, and to walk with sinners. He didn't stay up there. He came close, came down here. He is the Good Shepherd, a title no normal king would have wanted. He's the Suffering Servant, all the way to death on the cross.

Do you know Jesus like this? If you do, can you release your hold on your idols? Can you give in to Jesus with your sins, your worries, your hopelessness, your ceaseless strivings. Elisabeth Elliot said giving in is the hardest thing to give. Can you give in and give over to Jesus?

There is one more part, the "So what?" to this passage. In Isaiah 40:29–31, we read:

He gives power to the faint, and to him who has no might he increases strength. Even youths shall faint and be weary, and young men shall fall exhausted; but they who wait for the LORD shall renew their strength; they shall mount up with wings like eagles; they shall run and not be weary; they shall walk and not faint.

You're faint and have no might. You're tired, and you've spent your last bit of money. You don't have childcare. You don't have self-control late at night. You're worn out, and you feel blasted by all you have to do. I felt that way after General Assembly.

My grass needs seeded and watered (what's the use?!). My house needs to be scraped and painted, my trees need trimmed, and my garage needs to be organized. I think to myself, "I can do this. I should do this." And yet I feel like I don't have time or energy to start even one of these projects.

I don't know what is going on with you, but most of you have at least something where hope has died. You, even you, are faint and weary. You've got kids to entertain, mouths to feed, ministry to volunteer for, and extra income to make. Is there rest for the weary?

In 40:27, we read *"Why do you say, O Jacob, and speak, O Israel, 'My way is hidden from the LORD, and my right is disregarded by my God?'"* Do you feel that way? Are you tired and weary, thinking God has forgotten a certain area of your life and you've been disregarded? Do you think you could do a better job if you were in charge? Do you ever doubt?

Ortland instructs us:

One kind of doubt *struggles to believe* in view of the "slings and arrows of outrageous fortune." This kind of doubt is open to God's answers. It's willing to listen. The other kind of doubt *resists belief.* Even when good and sufficient reasons are offered, this kind of doubt folds its arms in defiance and says, "Nah! I still doubt it. And nothing you can say will satisfy me." That kind of doubt isn't even able to hear what God has to say.[9]

Which kind of doubter are you? Are you willing to hear God's answer? Are you struggling to believe but open to it? If so, I have a word for you and have been speaking to you words of life. Listen.

If you resist belief, then you aren't willing to hear God's answer.

You will go your own way. You may even blame me or the church or God.

But I have a word for you in the midst of destruction—listen, grasshopper.

If you are open to hear God, there is hope for those who wait on the Lord. Their strength will be renewed. They will soar. They will run. They will walk. Maybe not today but someday, and then it will be for forever.

The king is coming. He has come and will again. Jesus Christ is the King. The prophets spoke of him. Indeed, he is changing the topography of the world, through the "disrupting advance of salvation."[10] He is changing the lay of the land of depression, of pride, of troubled personalities, of difficult people. He is challenging the status quo and constructing a different way of life, one of the Lord's.

The creator of all the cosmos, the stars, and galaxies—this Creator King is coming. Long live the king!

What are we to do? Isaiah tells us we are to do the hardest thing —to wait.

Wait for the Lord. Waiting for the Lord is not killing time, but it is an eager longing, the suspenseful hope of something to come. One commentator writes:

> It isn't erratic bursts of hyperactivity within a general pattern of boredom. It is the steady, rugged progress, sustained by conviction that the display of God's glory in Christ is yours.[11]

I think this is why we see this pattern, which seems anticlimactic —soar, run, walk. The goal of the Christian life is to walk in faithfulness.

It's captured in the title of Eugene Peterson's book *A Long Obedience in the Same Direction*.[12] The pilgrimage of faith is one of hope in a promise yet to come. As we wait, we obey, and we expect. A life of faith is one of steady forward progress following the one whose resources are limitless.[13]

Are you willing to wait for God to show up on his terms? Or are you such a controlling person that you can't live on God's terms, you can't give in to him in *that* area? Oswald writes:

Those who give up their own frantic efforts to save themselves and turn expectantly to God will be able to replace or exchange their worn-out strength for new strength. How like God: he takes the useless and gives back the good.[14]

Perhaps even today you will see Jesus as the Comforting-Shepherd-Warrior-King, the one who saves sinners with double payment, more than you would expect. Maybe you could name some of your "I've made a lot of mistakes." You could look your idols in the eyes and see them for the counterfeit pretenders they are. You might understand your irritableness, moodiness, and unhappiness is a function of your heart not believing that you are truly loved in Christ alone and you're constantly searching for glory in others. You could stop thinking God will underwrite your worldliness and instead give in with everything in your life.

In Matthew 11:27–30, Jesus says:

> All things have been handed over to me by my Father, and no one knows the Son except the Father, and no one knows the Father except the Son and anyone to whom the Son chooses to reveal him. Come to me, all who labor and are heavy laden, and I will give you rest. Take my yoke upon you, and learn from me, for I am gentle and lowly in heart, and you will find rest for your souls. For my yoke is easy, and my burden is light.

He could blow you away like cut grass, weeds, or dandelion puffs. The grass withers and the flowers fade, but the Word of our God stands forever. Jesus is the Word of God made flesh, come to dwell among us, come to intercede for us, to make a propitiation for us, to raise again from the dead for us. He stands forever.

Jesus is the king. All things have been given to him alone. Do you know him? Has he revealed himself to you? If so, he offers you his comfort:

> Come to me, all who labor and are heavy laden, and I will give you rest. Take my yoke upon you, and learn from me, for I am gentle and lowly in heart, and you will find rest for your souls. For my yoke is easy, and my burden is light. (Matt. 11:20–30)

Jesus is the answer to these questions: How can we rest? How can we find peace? How can we be made right with God? What are we here for?

Jesus is able and willing to save you. Even you and me. Give in to him. Let the creator recreate you. May he make all things new again.

This greatness will never fade, will never be replaced, and will never get old. It's the greatness of a powerful, creative, redemptive, and rescuing love.

Sufjan finishes his song this way, and we can sing it with him:

> *you came to take us*
> *all things go, all things go*
> *to recreate us*
> *all things grow, all things grow*
> *we had our mindset*
> *(I made a lot of mistakes)*
> *all things know, all things know*
> *(I made a lot of mistakes)*
> *you had to find it*
> *(I made a lot of mistakes)*
> *all things go, all things go*
> *(I made a lot of mistakes)*

ISAIAH 42–43

A few years ago, a massive storm rolled over Oklahoma City. It was tornado season, and everyone was worried one might hit downtown and cause even more extensive damage than normal. We (the Servens) watched and tracked it, and it headed straight for our neighborhood. We were ready to get out!

So we packed up our family (and our dog), forced our eighty-year-old neighbor to get in the car with us, and we drove south along with everyone else in the city. We ended up at the Warren Theater since it had withstood the damage from an earlier powerful tornado. We knew it would be safe. We sat in the hallway with hundreds of other families, crying babies, and dogs.

The storm never funneled. Instead it parked itself in the same spot for several hours, dumping rain in only one location. Everyone lost power.

We made it home, glad to be away from another natural disaster.

What we hadn't realized was our basement had flooded, and our sump pump, quite naturally, doesn't work without electricity. The next morning, I had over two feet of cold water in my basement that had been sitting there for twelve hours.

I spent that day hauling water out with five-gallon buckets by hand. Over and over and over. From the basement, up the stairs, out the door, and down the street. It took a lot of work, and everything that had been down there was ruined.

I pay closer attention to our basement now when it rains.

That was not a great flood, but it cost a personal toll to me, however minor. I looked up some of the greatest floods and learned that in 1931, a flood came after a long drought in China.[1] Dams and levees broke, and over 70,000 square miles were flooded with ten to fifteen feet of water for three to six months. 140,000 people perished in the flood itself. It's estimated 3.7 million people died as a result in the nine months afterward.

I also looked up great fires.[2]

We've heard of the great Chicago fire in 1871, the one supposedly started by the cow in O'Leary's barn. 300 people died, and it left 90,000 homeless.

When Napoleon rolled into Moscow in 1812 to conquer the city, he didn't find any resistance, but there were small fires. The next day the fires consolidated into a roaring one that burned down three-quarters of the city and killed 12,000 people.

A huge earthquake started a fire in Tokyo in 1923. 38,000 people died directly from the fire, and 142,000 people died in the disaster combination. A typhoon blew in that spread the fire throughout the city.

And then there was my April dumpster fire. At around midnight, I put (relatively) hot coals into the dumpster because I wanted to be able to burn more wood outside and the bowl was full. That was a bad mistake.

Consider this a Public Service Announcement (one I bet you do not need).

Two days later (they had smoldered in there for two days), we heard what sounded like fireworks, and everything went dark in our house. We rushed outside, and found the dumpster had completely caught on fire. The flames had moved onto the wooden siding, which is where our electrical box was. We hosed it off, and the fire trucks were there within a few minutes.

Not only did I feel like an idiot, but this took nearly two months of work to fix. Now I'm happy to report—it's better than new!

Floods and fires. We may not encounter them often, but they wreak havoc in our lives. We're familiar with hearing about Hurricane Katrina, the Mississippi River, and the floods in Houston. We see pictures of wildfires every few months, and we know not to drive into smoke.

We have floods and fires in our own lives. We pray for rain, and then get too much of a good thing. When it rains, it pours. Fire is fine when it's contained in its proper place. When it gets out, it destroys. It goes wild, and we feel inadequate to stop its ravenous hunger.

Isaiah 43 says God is with us even in the floods and fires in our lives. I wish it said he'd stop them from happening. We're told someday he will, but we're not there yet. Until then, he says he's with us even in the floods and fires. He's with us in the great ones and in the small ones. Let's look and see how Isaiah 42–44 might matter to us now, just as it did then.

Our Problem—A Handicapped People

Sometimes it feels like God is mean. We've all thought that before, haven't we? We don't like the way he judges, rules, or takes territory. We feel like he's a tyrant, and we don't like his Old Testament ways.

Here's one perhaps mild example. In Isaiah 42:18–25, we read:

> *Hear, you deaf, and look, you blind, that you may see! Who is blind but my servant, or deaf as my messenger whom I send? Who is blind as my dedicated one, or blind as the servant of the Lord? He sees many things, but does not observe them; his ears are open, but he does not hear. The Lord was pleased, for his righteousness' sake, to magnify his law and make it glorious. But this is a people plundered and looted; they are all of them trapped in holes and hidden in prisons; they have become plunder with none to rescue, spoil with none to say, "Restore!" Who among you will give ear to this, will attend and listen for the time to come? Who gave up Jacob to the looter, and Israel to the plunderers?*
>
> *Was it not the Lord, against whom we have sinned, in whose ways they would not walk, and whose law they would not obey? So he poured on him the heat of his anger and the might of battle; it set him on fire all around, but he did not understand; it burned him up, but he did not take it to heart.*

He calls his people deaf and blind, and yet he calls them to see and hear. Is it fair to ask deaf people to hear or blind people to see? Isn't that pushing their noses into their infirmities? But here in the biblical text, they're deaf and blind by choice. They both can and can't see. God's pointing out the spiritual nature of their condition, and how they cannot see the reality of the world. They're missing out on all the senses and the fullness of life by rejecting God himself. They're worse off for it. God calls them to move in and move forward. There is more for them if they won't accept those limitations. Life can open up for them if they'll see and hear differently.

He keeps it up. He says the people knew from God what is right and good, but instead, they plundered and looted. So they're trapped and hidden in prisons.

One day I started in on some tree trimming[3] on a Friday at about 10:30am. I had just gotten set up when a man rode by me on his bicycle and asked if I needed help. He needed some money and said he would take whatever I could pay him. He wanted to buy his son a present for his birthday.

Over the next few hours, LeRoy told me his story. He'd been in and out of prison since he was eleven. He'd sold drugs, robbed people, and done everything short of violent crime (so he said). He told me he was now trying to live right and not do anyone any harm, which was a big change for him. He realized he had very few friends when he didn't have any money, but he was happier this way. He still missed the high rolling life sometimes, and he didn't like dumpster diving. But he didn't miss jail. And he was glad to be poor and forgiven by the grace of God.

[He might have been an angel.]

———

"They have become plunder with none to rescue, spoil with none to say, 'Restore!'" (Isa. 42:22). This is exactly the opposite of what we want at our church and in the Kingdom of God. None to rescue. None to restore. This is that antithesis of what we're about as the church of Jesus Christ. This is a rejection of the Gospel of grace and mercy. It's hell on earth.

God names his people in Isaiah 42. He reminds them Jacob and Israel are their names. They were called by God, set free, rescued, and restored. And yet, they had wandered away. God had saved them, and they had sinned against him. They stopped walking with and obeying him. They thought his rules and commandments were too much, were for their harm and not their good.

God judges this.

It's important to remember this assessment is for his own people. He's not talking about the Assyrians, Babylonians, Midionites, or Amalekites. He's not talking about Muslims, Buddhists, atheists, secular humanists, or anyone else. He's talking to us. To you if you are a Christian.

Ouch.

So let's take that seriously. Where am I deaf to God? To what am I blind to? How am I imprisoned instead of free? Am I more like Old LeRoy or New LeRoy? Do I want rescue and restoration, or am I happy to go my own way? Am I obeying God no matter what, or do I make excuses and allowances that perhaps God should see things my way?

If our purpose in life is to glorify God and enjoy him forever, how am I doing? Is this my daily mission?

Our Solution—A Powerful, Gracious, Personal, Immanuel God

I hope you sense the dilemma. God has made a covenant to love his people. He set it up, and he's committed to it. We the people have agreed to it, and yet we fail again and again. Not "them." Us.

Be careful about the dreaded *they*.

They don't worship correctly. They don't run their families right, and they don't love their children well. They don't follow the laws or respect authority. They don't express themselves. They don't communicate. They don't care about the environment. They don't care about the poor or unborn, or taxes, or healthcare, or schools, or choice, or mask mandates, or vaccinations, or… you name it. As long as you're squishy about the rules, you can get off the hook and find yourself on the positive side of the ledger.

But God doesn't agree. He's not impressed with either their goodness or yours. But we're talking about ours, not theirs.

You've got to see yourself here or else you're doomed in the blindness and deafness, in the imprisonment. You'll be in the sunken place forever. You've got to wake up and see the reality of things. You've got to get out.

Our problem is now God's remedy. We didn't change, shape up, or get with the program, and yet God continues to show his love. This is the grace of God. It was then, and it is now.

How is this grace communicated to them and to us? By six great themes.

Creation and Redemption

"Fear not, for I have redeemed you; I have called you by name, you are mine" (Isa. 43:1). Creation isn't in the forefront of this passage, but it's assumed. God's people would know the Genesis story. They would know they were created by God and named by him. Every person is made in the image of God. We bear his glory, however marred. We're glorious ruins. The most hideous sinner still deserves respect as a person, a creation of God unlike any other. We're a called people. We are his. We may have rebelled, but we are still his.

As such, God breaks into our deaf world and into our blindness. He's the preceding action, first cause, prime mover, and the creator yet again. We're responding to him. He has every right to leave us alone, but he moves into our lives with tenderness and faithfulness.

He says, "You are mine. I am yours. I created you, and I have redeemed you. I will not forsake you. I will be with you."

The power of the one who created the universe is here in his lavish generosity. The king is on the move. He's gathering people from all directions—north, south, east, and west.

God is rescuing and ransoming his people. That's what kings do when the ones they love are in trouble. They go out and rescue them to bring them back home.

Protection

When you pass through the waters, I will be with you; and through the rivers, they shall not overwhelm you; when you walk through fire you shall not be burned, and the flame shall not consume you. (Isa. 43:2)

This is the moment in the superhero movie where the person in trouble fully expects to be rescued. For whatever reason, by the culmination of a series of events, she's in trouble. He needs saving. She doesn't want to be there.

The bad guy has him or her in his clutches. Evil seems like it is going to win. Will the hero arrive in time? We've seen movies where she doesn't. Will this be one of those?

We think our movie will end badly. We take every moment as our last. We've been taught we must always succeed, always triumph, and we must always get saved. Bad times should always be far from us.

Isaiah is more like a high school coach here. Name your sport—volleyball, rowing, cross country, football, basketball, the debate team, or ballet.

Isaiah has gathered the freshmen together before the season starts, and he says to those who've shown up. His speech goes:

Team! We're going to win! You're going to be champions by the end of our four years together. We're going to take our lumps. We'll get knocked down. You'll get made fun of. You'll suffer. You'll puke from wind sprints, five-mile runs, stadium steps, drills, burpees, and you'll probably hate me at times. We'll fight. I'll disappoint you. We'll make mistakes. We'll lose games by a ton, and we'll lose at the last second. We'll want to spend time away from each other. But know this—I'm with you. We'll go through what feels like hell together. We'll have each others' backs. I'll have yours. I trust in you. I know what I'm doing. If you trust in me, we'll get there. We'll be champions!

This is *Hoosiers* or *Remember the Titans*, or *Miracle* for USA Hockey.

This is *Field of Dreams, Major League,* or *A League of Their Own.* It's David over Goliath again and again. It's the way God works.

The anti-hero goes through the wilderness. He goes through the fire, the flood, through being sold into slavery, being the runt of the litter, being the ugly duckling, and through being the self-righteous murderous Pharisee.

God doesn't spare us this training ground. We may feel pushed under and burned up. But we'll not be overwhelmed. Perhaps we should stop describing our lives that way. We're always over-whelmed, and I'm a prime culprit for overusing that description.

God tells us that we shall not be burned or consumed. We are more than conquerors in Christ who loves us.

What are your floods and fires? Where do you need God to be with you? At home? At school? At work? In your marriage? In your room? When you take the bus? When you got fired? When you're bored? When you're pushed to the limit of your patience? With your past? In the hospital room? Late at night?

God is there. He's with you.

Isaiah's point here is that if you are loved like that you have nothing to fear. You're no longer a worthless grasshopper. You're an heir, a son, a daughter, a bride. You're beloved, cherished, and sung over with gladness.

Witnesses

"You are my witnesses," declares the Lord, "and my servant whom I have chosen." (Isa. 43:10)

Fear is crippling, but we are witnesses. It can be tough to feel so alone without God.

And then it's also tough to think God was there, and he didn't stop it—whatever that "it" is for you—from happening. He could have stopped that fire from catching or spreading. He could have held back those waters since controls the winds and the waves.

But he didn't stop the bad things. I was touched, and he was there. I had that heart attack, and he was there. I got that sickness, and he was there. The freak accident happened, and he was there. I lost the baby, and he was there. He was there that awful night, all throughout that awful marriage, and in my awful life.

The Bible is filled with laments. It's perfectly acceptable to raise our cries up to God in protest. We can scream and shout, raise our fists, give him the finger, and wonder at his ways.

What you see is this progression of a threat, and then a lament, and then sometime later (fast or slow, minutes or decades) a cry of salvation turns into a song of confidence. We go from "I am afraid," to hearing "Do not fear," to shouting from the rooftops "I will not fear."

We feel forsaken (*"My God, my God why have you forsaken me?"* Ps. 22:1), but then we feel assured God is with us wherever we go, even in the valley of the shadow of death (Ps. 23).[4] We feel alone, but God tells us he is with us, and then we understand it somehow. There is a dramatic leap from lament to songs of trust as God comforts his people (Isa. 40:1).

Then we become his witnesses, saying there is no savior but God. He is our deliverer, rescuer, strong tower, and our mighty fortress. In God we trust. Not in horses or chariots, 401ks, strength, beauty, charm, IQs, EQs, Myers Briggs, Enneagrams, neighborhoods, GPAs, fitness, marital status, politics, or... anything.

Other gods have their witnesses too. Everyone stands on something. It might be family values, environmental reclamation, education advancement. our good names, creating wealth for the next generation, the freedom to be me, or breaking the rules by going against the man.

Or a closet full of real idols. Or secular humanism or science. Or a loose Buddhism. Or Marduk or Baal. Call it whatever you want.

God's strange strategy is to rely on us as his witnesses. He's accused of being a liar, and yet he uses us—Jacobs, Josephs, Abrahams, Isaacs, Leahs, Rachels, and... Ugandas, Shrekas, Kats, Caylees, Julies, Annas, Beckys, Catherines, Anna Ruths, Codys, Tims, Matts, Mikes, Elijahs, Naviirs, Georges, Jakes, Joshes, Bobbys, Dougs....

He does this to show forth his goodness and glory. What kind of a plan is that? He uses feeble people. He uses the weak and foolish. He's chosen you and me to be his witnesses to his work and person.

Present Future Glory

I am the Lord, your Holy One, the Creator of Israel, your King." (Isa. 43:15)

"Behold, I am doing a new thing; now it springs forth, do you not perceive it? (Isa. 43:19)

We stand as witnesses to God, so we tell our stories of rescue. We tell of God's presence not his absence. We tell of his mysterious ways, trusting in his plan that we don't fully understand. We find our stories in his story of creation, fall, redemption, and restoration.

And he stands with us, over and over. Our creator made us, and even though we have rejected him, he is our Lord. He's holy. He can measure the universe with the span of his hand and hold the waters in his palm. He can measure the sands on the shore and the hairs on your head. He's the king who has come and will come again.

This Mighty God, King of Kings, and Lord of Lords will defeat all his and our foes. Our enemies seem so strong, but they are not invincible. The Assyrians left town, and the Babylonians were defeated (and are no more). Rome fell.

Dynasties fade away, and dictators die off. Hitler was defeated, and the Berlin Wall was torn down. Rocky brought the Cold War to an end. ISIS will not last. Whatever you think of presidents and governors, their terms have limits. We'll get another one soon enough.

But our God reigns. We can't only be brave. We have to be able to defeat the enemy, and God says he can and will do it.

These people aren't hearing this message ready to get in their air-conditioned cars for a drive back for Sunday brunch, a nap, some baseball, and yard work. They're in exile. They're listening on a long journey back home to Jerusalem, a trek of 500 to 900 miles depending on where they've been exiled. They have four months of walking ahead of them. When they arrive, they're going to find a devastated land awaiting them. After an exhausting and dangerous journey, they'll have to rebuild everything from scratch.

They need to hear and believe God makes all things new. His goodness springs forth. The wilderness, desert, and city are all conquered already. They need to claim the land and build up the new Jerusalem in his spirit, in his goodness. It's a new, second exodus.

God still makes all things new. He can rebuild your life now. From the ashes and the ruins. From your bad decisions, past mistakes, wrong lovers, tragic grades, low pay, unfortunate job, lack of education, wrong side of town, fatherlessness (whether its literal or figurative), overbearing parents, felony offenses, first marriage and subsequent divorce, loneliness at night, and whatever else you've done or left undone.

He can go ahead of you and make a way. He can resurrect your love. He can walk before you with your dad or son or friend or neighbor. He can go ahead of you in your business. He can calm your anxious heart. He can slay the Assyrians! He can restore Jerusalem from the Babylonians! He can bring a man from the dead! He can resurrect from the dead himself, conquering death! The king will come again, long live the king!

Blessing

> But now hear, O Jacob my servant, Israel whom I have chosen! Thus says the Lord who made you, who formed you from the womb and will help you: Fear not, O Jacob my servant, Jeshurun whom I have chosen. For I will pour water on the thirsty land, and streams on the dry ground; I will pour my Spirit upon your offspring, and my blessing on your descendants. They shall spring up among the grass like willows by flowing streams This one will say, "I am the Lord's," another will call on the name of Jacob, and another will write on his hand, "The Lord's," and name himself by the name of Israel. (Isa. 44:1–5)

If God can do all that, it means he blesses his children whom he's chosen and loves. He made you. He has called, rescued, and helped you. Don't be afraid. We may run sprints til we puke, but there is an end-goal in sight, the blessing of a day at the podium, of winning that last game and being crowned champions.

These are impossible prayer requests being answered. Water on a thirsty land, streams on the dry ground. His Spirit poured out on our children and our children's children, springing up in lush goodness, claiming God as their Father, even marking themselves and naming themselves the people of God. That's what we want.

Our faith isn't merely intellectual. To be sure, it is intellectual. We use our brains to figure this out. But all knowledge is relational. These aren't theorems we're postulating. It's not a logic puzzle or a really tough Sudoku.

God is a person. Jesus was a person, both God and man. The Holy Spirit is a person. We're God's people, his children. We're Jesus' bride. We're united together in the body of Christ.

We need God to help us to flourish, to make things right. We want flourishing for ourselves, our church, our children, our city, state, nation, and world. It's exciting when we see things happen, when miracles occur, when joy breaks forth from sadness, when light shines in the darkness.

May the Lord bless us. May the Lord bless you.

Forgiveness

I, I am he who blots out your transgressions for my own sake, and I will not remember your sins. (Isa. 43:25)

We get to the big finish. A lot of people are mad at God. He seems mean and nasty. He punishes sin, blots out nations, and judges the wicked. It makes sense to be angry at someone so powerful and so awful (if it's an accurate assessment).

We've been taught that we must be true to ourselves, we must not tell others what to do, and we cannot ever question what someone thinks is right and wrong. These are truths in our society right now. Be all you can be. Be true to yourself. Find yourself. Find your tribe.

We can affirm some of this. We're all created in the image of God. We want people to flourish. We want to give respect and honor to everyone. We love and cherish people and God's creation.

But there's this sticking point. There's something called sin that gets in the way. What if deep down in the deepest part of you, you're a sinner? What if your true self is a liar? Or a thief? Or a murderer

Or an embezzler? What if all you want to do is watch pornography all day? What if your true self is someone who doesn't go to school, drops out in third grade and watches day-time television every day? What if your inner self is morbidly obese, bulimic, anorexic? What if your true self hates yourself, or hates men, or women, Black people, White people. Latinos. or Asian-Americans What if your true self is a polygamist or a child abuser?

Christianity has always said there's a moral authority—God determines what is right and wrong. We're supposed to think what he thinks and live our lives in a way that pleases and honors him. That's the good life. That's what is right and true.

Yes, we fail all the time, but there's something to shoot for. It's not all up for grabs and up to us to determine.

The other part of the equation is that God forgives. Hallelujah!

When I peer into my heart of hearts and look deep down at my true nature, I see a sinner. I see deep, persistent sin. I see a person who often doesn't even know or understand how he's been shaped by his culture, nation, upbringing, gender, age, Whiteness, and even his height, weight, and abilities. I almost always give myself the benefit of the doubt, but perhaps that's another indication of a real blindness to myself.

I need help! I'm mean, sarcastic, selfish, and greedy. I cuss too much and drink too much. I overestimate myself and think too highly of myself. I'm proud. I'm racist, however unintentionally. I treat people poorly and am a bad friend. I don't love my neighbors. I'm a Pharisee. I'm the other two characters in the parable of the Good Samaritan, the ones who don't stop to help.

This is a pastor speaking!

We can always try to do better. We can work harder to eliminate the bad and accentuate the good.

However, what we really need is—forgiveness. We need someone who knows it all and still loves us. Someone who doesn't blot us out, but who writes our names in the book of life, who gives us new names, who calls us his Beloved, who takes our debt, who pays our price, who sets us free, who forgives!

I'm thankful God delivers us.

This happens through Jesus Christ. He was smitten, stricken, and afflicted so you could be set free. He was wiped out so you could be brought in. He was cast out to the Place of the Skull, so you could be picked up and taken into the courts of the king. By his wounds you are healed. His cursing is your blessing, and his shame is your glory. His nakedness on the cross is what allows you to be dressed in the finest linens.

We can't just do better. We're sinners!

We need outside help. We need a new nature.

We have that in Christ. We're told we're new creations, the old is gone and the new has come. We can be a forgiven people, thrilled to be both known and loved. We don't have to have secrets any more. We can be free. You were worth saving!

In his song "More Than I Can Bear," Kirk Franklin sings:

> *I've gone through the fire*
> *And I've been through the flood*
> *I've been broken into pieces*
> *Seen lightnin' flashin' from above*
> *But through it all I remember*
> *That He loves me And He cares*
> *And He'll never put more on me*
> *Than I can bear*

Marvin Gaye and Tammi Terrell sing:

> *Remember the day I set you free*
> *I told you you could always count on me darling*
> *From that day on, I made a vow*
> *I'll be there when you want me*
> *Some way, some how*
> *Oh baby there ain't no mountain high enough*
> *Ain't no valley low enough*
> *Ain't no river wide enough*
> *To keep me from getting to you babe*

We could name other songs that have this theme. There are plenty of them.

But it's Isaiah who teaches us:

Fear not, for I have redeemed you; I have called you by name, you are mine. When you pass through the waters, I will be with you; and through the rivers, they shall not overwhelm you; when you walk through fire you shall not be burned and the flame shall not consume you. For I am the Lord your God, the Holy One of Israel, your Savior. (Isa. 43:2)

ISAIAH 44

We're looking at and thinking about what it's like when you're in the presence of greatness. For Isaiah 44, I'm (Doug) wondering about what it's like to meet one of your idols. What if you get to meet someone you have always dreamed of meeting? The Pioneer Woman for Natalie. Mark McGuire for me. Mike Gundy for Matt. Justin Bieber for you.

Meeting someone you have idolized is always an interesting experience. I once stood in the urinal stall next to R. C. Sproul, which I guess is mildly disturbing. I hung out with Tim Keller.

Sometimes it's great (Natalie and The Pioneer Woman). Sometimes you feel stupid (me and Mark McGuire). And sometimes the person you're meeting just isn't what you thought he or she would be. Maybe it's an off day. Maybe the person is normal, and you built her up in your mind; there's no way she can compare.

I heard a great story about this. A man was with his kids in the airport, and he sees Val Kilmer. Now maybe he didn't idolize Val Kilmer, but one of the Batman movies had come out, and Val was pretty big, and there they were in a chance meeting. So the man went up to Val with his kids in tow. As he approached, he watched Val pretend to answer a call on his cell phone. He stood there for a bit longer, and then asked politely, "Could I get a quick autograph for my kids, Val?" Val didn't want to talk and was still pretending to make chit chat on the phone. The man asked again, in a hushed tone, wanting to respect Val's privacy but also hoping to get an autograph.

What happens next?

In this passage I want you to imagine approaching your idol. Maybe not Val Kilmer. Who or what would your top idol be? Who would you dream of meeting? Magic Johnson? Beyonce? Chef Bobby Flay? Richard Branson? Garth Brooks? Have you bumped into someone famous? My dad walked into an elevator with the Michigan State basketball coach Tom Izzo, and Dan Serven was thrilled.

We're using Isaiah as our guide. We can't cover every chapter, but we're trying to hit the highlights to see what this ancient book says to us today. Isaiah seems like he's speaking right to us in all that is going on in our lives too. It's our job to figure out what that means and how we can respond to him. It's our job to look for Jesus in the Scriptures.

This passage is like an American Idol contest. God is looking for entries for our favorite entertainers. He's going to put them on stage and judge them for all to see who is the winner. We need to pull forward from Isaiah 41:21–23, which reads:

> Set forth your case, says the LORD; bring your proofs, says the King of Jacob. Let them bring them, and tell us what is to happen. Tell us the former things, what they are, that we may consider them, that we may know their outcome; or declare to us the things to come. Tell us what is to come hereafter, that we may know that you are gods; do good, or do harm, that we may be dismayed and terrified.

God asks for a public forum, a debate, a contest. "Set forth your case," he says. "Bring your proofs." One of the key characteristics he's looking for is the ability to tell what is to happen in the future and to explain the things of the past.

That makes sense. If a God is powerful and able to sit above the world in any sort of majesty, he should be able to shape the outcome of things to come. Will Yahweh be able to do this? After all, he's in the competition too. Let's see.

Our Problem—Boredom and Idol Worship

We have a lot of problems. I'm first in line with mine. And like a good prophet, pastor, and friend, Isaiah doesn't pull back from talking about our what's going wrong. He's giving his assessment. He's analyzed the results and is ready to make suggestions about what can be improved. Like a property assessor. Like intake at the new gym you just joined. Like pulling your car into the garage for a checkup.

The first problem is boredom. That might surprise you. And wow, is this a modern problem or what? Get your fidget-spinners ready.

What do you do when you get bored? I have a friend who told me about a classmate he had in seminary who he'd watch every day. It was remarkable because this person picked at stuff on his body all throughout class. The whole class picking, picking, picking. He especially liked to dig into his ears with a paperclip.

I haven't seen this particular manifestation of boredom, but what do you do when you get bored? Take off? Daydream? Just leave? Do you fall asleep? You start checking your phone, don't you?

Boredom is common in our cynical, jaded, over-stimulated society. Whereas Americans used to be able to listen regularly to a three-hour speech, now if it isn't expressed in fifteen-second sound bites with eye-popping video, we tune out. Movies need to be ninety minutes. Books have to move at a fast clip. Nothing can drag, especially not church. Entertain me!

This isn't a new phenomenon. Isaiah speaks of it in his time as well. God's people are filled with effort, but they are empty of joy and passion. He writes that God says:

Yet you did not call upon me, O Jacob; but you have been weary of me, O Israel!
You have not brought me your sheep for burnt offerings, or honored me with your
sacrifices. I have not burdened you with offerings, or wearied you with
frankincense. (Isa.44:22–23)

The contrast is:
You have wearied of me / I have not wearied you.
This is one of the problems we have. Many people still go to

worship, but they attend in body and not in spirit. It's like the practice alone will save them. They attend every week, week after week, because that is what they do. They've been taught to. They're good people. And good people go to church (though fewer people agree with this logic).

Where is the passion in that? Where's the excitement of the drama of redemption? It's gone, robbed in a ritualistic, weary worship.

The other response to weariness is an opposite one. We just stop going altogether. I'm tired of this, so I'm out.

This is becoming more and more common, isn't it? In some ways it's good because people are more honest about their faith practices and church attendance. They just don't go at all anymore. What's the point?

At OU where I was a campus minister from 2001–2011, some 80 percent of students claim to be Christians. They would mark Christianity on a box, self-reporting their faith stance. But I would guess on any given week you would only find 1000–2000 involved in any Christian activity like Bible study or church worship. So of the 16,000 who claim Christianity, 14–15,000 of them have opted out of getting together to sing hymns, study the Bible, take the Lord's Supper, or corporately confess sin.

The statistics in Oklahoma City say 65 percent of the people in our city do not attend church. That's a lot of non-church attendance in a city and a state that seems extremely conservative and Christian.

Maybe they have good reasons—too tired on Sunday mornings. There are better things to do. Maybe they've been church-hurt, which is extremely common. Perhaps they think they'll get back into it later in life when things matter more (a very dangerous way of thinking about anything).

Church is simply too boring. I often think the church I pastor has got to be better than staying at home. I'm sure sometimes we aren't. And people don't like being talked down to. They don't like the moralism, the hypocrisy, the lack of conversation and hospitality. No one does.

Whatever the reason, they don't think they need it. They're probably bored.

Why is church worth your time? So many of your friends, even Christian ones, don't think it is. I'll bet sometimes you agree with them. You wonder why you've come, why you return, and if you will. Do you feel this way?

We'll get back to this boredom dilemma, but the second problem is our idol worship. We read about this all the way through Isaiah, but particularly right here in 44:6–20.

Tim Keller helps us address idols in our lives and hearts—how to expose them and how to get rid of them (painfully). Let me summarize the way he talks about this.

Idols aren't the things you go buy at Raven's Feather, pick up at the flea market, or come home with from other exotic countries. Sure you can buy those, and that would be a literal interpretation.

We may not have these actual totems, but we still have functional idols. The real idols of our lives and hearts are the good things we take and make ultimate, things we *have* to have. They become what we live for. They become our gods. Again, in and of themselves, they are fine things. There is nothing wrong with sex, beauty, success, money, esteem, knowledge, or anything else—except when they become our all in all, the thing we cannot live without.

I cannot live without _____. What goes in the blank for you?

Keller writes about power and influence over others. Perhaps that's what gives life meaning. It's what gives me worth. He writes:

I only have worth if I am loved, respected, and approved of. I have to have this particular quality of life. Life only has meaning if I attain and continue with this body image and kind of look. I only have worth if I'm able to get mastery in my life over this area. Life only has worth if these people are dependent on me. Life is worth living if there is someone to protect me and keep me safe. I only have worth if I'm completely free from obligations and responsibilities. I must be productive and get a lot done. I must be recognized for my accomplishments and excel in my career. I'm a worthwhile person if I adhere to my religious code and accomplish its ideals. I'm worthwhile if I am totally independent of organized religion and follow my self-made morality. I only have worth if my race and culture is ascending and recognized as superior. Life has meaning if I'm a member of this particular social or professional group or if that group lets me in. Life only has meaning if my children/parents/family are happy. Life only has meaning if I'm hurting or in a problem because then I feel noble and worthy of love. I only have worth if my political party is making progress in power.

What cannot you not live without? Your kids? Spouse? Health? Vacation? House? Freedom?

Isaiah communicates this same message, albeit with ancient language. Isaiah exposes the emptiness and absurdity of idolatry through verses 9–17. He speaks of the futility of idolatry, commenting that it makes no sense. Idolatry brings no profit to the soul. Idolatry can be commended only on the basis of blind ignorance. Idolaters are ignorant and blind. Idolatry is logically indefensible. Idolatry is dead, meaningless, profitless, and it grips the idolater in a deep choke hold.

Isaiah says idols cannot rise above their makers, which seems pretty obvious when you're talking about wood, stone, and metal. Someone has to make it. Then why would you bow down and worship it?

But idols do even more insidious things. They cannot undeceive. Instead, they lead to degradation and degeneration.

Verse 19 is a devastating analysis of the fallen mind. In 44:20, the idolater is hooked on idolatry. It blinds us.

It is astonishing how absurd idolatry is, but it is even more astonishing that we don't see it. This can only be explained by its power which gets added to the deceitfulness of our hearts (Jer. 17:9). Only a deluded heart can explain our idolatry—because it is so absurd. Idols are lies. They preserve the illusion of self-control, but their limits are your limits. They have no power because we who have made them have no power.

I'm trying to say anything at all can be an idol. Sure money, sex, and power may be the most common, but these work themselves out in a million different ways.

I read a book called *The Billionaire's Vinegar* that detailed the possible and alleged forgery market in wine trading. I know it's hard to realize people pay more than the $5 Boone's Farms, but indeed they do. I'm not even talking about a good box Shiraz.

At this exquisite level, it's difficult to figure out if these are fakes because people can mix old wines and new wines, make bottles look old, and "discover" these bottles in long, lost cellars. And then the ultimate—you drink the evidence, so it's gone forever.

The Forbes family paid $265,000 at auction for a bottle of 1789 wine supposedly once owned by Thomas Jefferson. There's a certain prestige about owning this bottle. In the wine world, this bottle is legendary. It also just might have been a fake. It could have been table wine for all anyone knows.

Idols are good things made ultimate. Wine. Family. Kids. Marriage. Relationships. Race. Culture. Politics. Safety. Security. Work. Comfort. Our intellects. Health. Ability to make money. Motherhood. Beauty. Fame.

Where have you spent a fortune of time, energy, or money? Think about this—where does the bulk of your time, money, and attention go? What are the top candidates?

What makes you angry? What is the thing you have to have?

———

Remember the man who encountered his idol Val Kilmer at the airport? He identified him, approached him, and Val wasn't doing it for him.

Val pretended not to hear him speak. He didn't want to sign an autograph, and I think what happened next was a Gospel response in light of our discussion here in Isaiah 44. The man looked at Val Kilmer and said, "I'm sorry to have to do this to you."

Then he turned around in the airport and shouted, "Hey everybody! Look, *it's Val Kilmer!*"

As he walked away, he winked at Val, who was instantly surrounded. Instead of three people wanting an autograph, he had three hundred. And he was really not happy then.

This man exposed his idol. And he walked away from him.

How does God help us to do that very thing?

God's Provision—Forgiveness and Refreshment

So we're in pretty bad shape here. The Bible doesn't say God saves good people. It says he saves bad people, and that is good news for sure because we're in the bad people group.

How does he rescue us?

First, he offers us forgiveness. Hallelujah, for we desperately need it!

We read:

> You have not bought me sweet cane with money, or satisfied me with the fat of your sacrifices. But you have burdened me with your sins; you have wearied me with your iniquities. "I, I am he who blots out your transgressions for my own sake, and I will not remember your sins." (Isa. 44:24–25)

The contrast this time is:

You have wearied me / I blot out your transgressions.

This is truly amazing. After acknowledging our boredom, inadequacy, sinfulness, and how wearisome those things are to him, God says he will forgive us. Indeed, "God locates his very identity in blotting out our sins and remembering them no more."[1]

This is the Gospel for us. God saves sinners! And yet, something inside us doesn't want grace. We want to justify ourselves, at least a little bit. That's why, with great irony, God invites us to come up with something in ourselves that deserves his mercy. He says, *"Put me in remembrance; let us argue together; set forth your case, that you may be proved right"* (Isa. 43:26).

What do we deserve? What would you come up with in this argument, this case before God? Hire the best lawyer and try it out. We say:

> Uh, God, I have never.... Well, God, I, um, help people sometimes.... God, I.....

We are left undone if we think about it for even a second. We have no case. Not before a holy God. Commentator Oswalt writes:

He's willing to be reminded of anything in their favor that they think he may have forgotten. The tone here is heavily ironic, and as such it directly addresses the fundamental problem. We humans do not like grace; we like to feel that we deserve everything we get. We want to be able to say that our good behavior has earned favorable treatment for us before the bar of God.[2]

But that isn't grace then, is it? Grace is unmerited favor. The unconditional grace of God is in view here.

God forgives us for his own name's sake. Commentator Motyer writes:

> Note that there is no connecting word between this verse (25) and 22–24. There is no logic whereby we might connect sin with forgiveness, nor does the Lord explain himself. The logic whereby the offended God is the forgiving God is hidden in his heart.[3]

Remember, the people who were likely reading this in the past were in actual physical national bondage. God tells them that captivity wasn't their root problem. It was the sin that caused the bondage in the first place. They might get released and still not get it. God had to forgive sin, not just change their circumstances.

Look at us. We have so much peace and so many freedoms, and yet we still fashion idols all the time. God, forgive us!

God also offers incredible refreshment.

When we look at the first part of Isaiah 44, we see refreshment comes by God's Spirit alone:

> But now hear, O Jacob my servant, Israel whom I have chosen! Thus says the Lord who made you, who formed you from the womb and will help you: Fear not, O Jacob my servant, Jeshurun whom I have chosen. For I will pour water on the thirsty land, and streams on the dry ground; I will pour my Spirit upon your offspring, and my blessing on your descendants. They shall spring up among the grass like willows by flowing streams. This one will say, "I am the Lord's," another will call on the name of Jacob, and another will write on his hand, "The Lord's," and name himself by the name of Israel. (Isa. 44:1–5)

It is amazing that nothing comes prior to this declaration. Instead of blotting them out, he takes away their sins. God himself is what saves us.

We need vacations. We need naps, the Sabbath, a bath with a glass of wine, a day of peace and quiet, a good meal and conversation, and a clean house.

These fill our cups. But we must continue to press into our need for the Lord, and he alone can give us ultimate refreshment.

The result of God's remedy is an enthusiasm for God's name alone. He's number one, and he's certainly not boring!

There is almost a competition to see who can be numbered as a person of God. People are lining up at the tattoo parlor to get "The Lord's" inked on their bodies. Israelites are becoming true Israelites. Churchgoers are becoming Christians, and Christians start going to church because they love it there.

The question is—Is that true for you?

Perhaps you've grown up hearing about Bible and Jesus, singing hymns, taking communion, and repeating the Lord's prayer. You may have grown up in a conservative, fundamentalist, or moralistic church. You also may have grown up in a liberal, traditional, or contemporary church. Yet, there is an astonishing lack of enthusiasm for God, for Jesus, for the Holy Spirit, for the Word of God.

One of the men who taught me the Bible was Vern Steiner in Lincoln, Nebraska. He told me the church he pastored before he moved was so taken by the Scriptures, they asked if they could lengthen the service so he could teach longer. They wanted more. They wanted to learn.

Are you quenched of your thirst by the Bible? Do you have a hunger for the word like that? Do you long for Christian fellowship? Would you sacrifice to go to prayer? Do you seek spiritual refreshment? When we see our sin finished and a new life imparted, we must see a personal response. Have you responded to the Gospel today? Have you gone cold?

Do you need forgiveness and refreshment today? I sure do. I'm a sinner with idols, and I need to be saved by grace. And I look forward to walking in complete freedom with Christ in his day and in his world. I am so thankful when I get tastes and glimpses of that in this one too.

How is it possible?

Because Jesus took our boredom and our idolatry onto himself. He was never bored with the Father. He delighted in God at all times. Can you imagine that? He never ignored him, never left him. He listened and loved the Father.

The people Jesus led and talked to wanted him to be a certain way. He could have been that way, been just like any other god or leader or super power or guru. Satan tempted him to do that very thing, to use his power for his own sake. But he wouldn't do it. The Jews wanted him to be the king and Messiah they wanted, to drive the Romans into the sea, to take over and demolish their enemies. The Romans just wanted him to go away. They could tolerate gods. After all they had a ton of them. But their gods didn't say and do things like Jesus said and did.

Jesus is the reason God forgives and refreshes. Our boredom and our idolatry were taken by him, and he gives us his never-ending passion for God alone. God sees Jesus when he looks at us, if we are found in him.

God's Promise—I Will Be with You

God also gives us a promise in this passage. You can find it in the beginning of chapter 43:

> But now thus says the Lord, he who created you, O Jacob, he who formed you, O Israel: "Fear not, for I have redeemed you; I have called you by name, you are mine. When you pass through the waters, I will be with you; and through the rivers, they shall not overwhelm you; when you walk through fire you shall not be burned, and the flame shall not consume you." (Isa. 43:1–3)

God says he will be with us. He says that all throughout the Scriptures, and it is a promise that many have held onto even through the worst circumstances.

I have to be honest—I can't totally explain it in a way you or I would like.

It might sound like God says nothing bad will happen to you. The rivers won't overwhelm you. The fire won't burn you. The flames won't consume you. But then when I put that together with the rest of Scripture and the overwhelming experience of Christians throughout time, we know that can't be what it's saying. God actually sends his people into waters, fire, and flames. He doesn't say you won't pass through the water, or rivers, or fires, or flames. He says, "When you do, I'll be with you."

Faithful, loving Christians have been burned at the stake and sent to the dogs. They've been imprisoned and enslaved. They've been run over and mowed down. They've been ignored and written off. They've been beheaded, lynched, and shot. They've been evicted, falsely accused, and deprived of opportunities.

God doesn't prevent sadness from his people, so we naturally think this faith thing must not work. God's promise must fail. We want him to keep the bad stuff away from us, and in the way our minds work, that makes a ton of sense.

Because there is a payoff that way. We end up getting what we really want after all. We think believing in God gets us safety. Believing in God gets us security. Believing in God gets us prosperity. This is the way we think. Muslims think this way too. If you prosper, that means God loves you. It's his way of showing that you are walking on the right path. If you suffer, it means God is mad at you.

It makes sense to us too. I talked with a friend who had given up on God. Why? Because after all his years of walking with God, he still got his dreams crushed and nothing worked out the way he wanted. He was done with Christianity if that was all it could do for him. He was just as happy without God as with God in his life.

Do you hear it? Do you hear the thing that lies under the thing? It wasn't God he wanted. He was using God to get the life he wanted. When he had that taken away, when the dream life was stripped out, and all he had was God— he didn't want it.

Christianity is full of death and suffering. Jesus said he came not to be served but to serve and to give his life as a ransom for many. Jesus said the loser is the winner. The one who loses his life will gain it. You can have the whole world but lose your very soul.

But that's just it. Jesus is the answer to this. God didn't prevent bad things from happening to Jesus, his son, the most perfect person of all time. He sent him all the wrath he had, all the way to the hell of the cross. Jesus took it all, all the fury of God. And what was Jesus' name? Immanuel, God with us. God sent his very own son for us. He is with us. He came to our neighborhood, town, to our very lives. That is a tremendous promise after all, and a redemptive one.

He promises to be with us. Not to keep all the bad away from us. But to bring the things in our lives that will bring us the closest to him. He did that to his people in this very book, sending them to exile and driving them to himself.

If you're like me, you don't really appreciate this promise very much. You think, "You'll be with me God?... uh... cool... okay.... Can I get something else too, something maybe a little more tangible?"

God says, "I'll still be with you." It's his promise.

Our Response—Awakening

What is our response to all this? It should be both a personal and a universal awakening.

We read in chapter 44:

> Remember these things, O Jacob, and Israel, for you are my servant; I formed you; you are my servant; O Israel, you will not be forgotten by me. I have blotted out your transgressions like a cloud and your sins like mist; return to me, for I have redeemed you. Sing, O heavens, for the Lord has done it; shout, O depths of the earth; break forth into singing, O mountains, O forest, and every tree in it! For the Lord has redeemed Jacob, and will be glorified in Israel. (Isa. 44:21–23)

What should we do as we see our need for him and his provision and promises for us?

Remember

Look back. Remember your need for redemption, God's pledge of forgiveness, and the certainty of his promise that God is the only God. God's people should ponder the truth they know.

Return

Commentator Alex Moytner writes:

> Coming back in repentance is not a good deed rewarded by redemption; the redemption has already taken place, opening the door for a return, making it both possible and effective, but which has been made for them.

Sing

Again, Motyner: "The picture of those who enter, with responsive joy, into a salvation to which they have made no contribution."[4]

Christianity is God to the rescue. He is the one who turns things around, who delivers us. Moytner writes:

> The idolater has been busy fashioning his idol but Israel has been fashioned by the Lord; the idolater is bound to his idol but Israel is the Lord's bondman; the idolater prayed pathetically, save me but to Israel the Lord says, I have redeemed you; the idolater bowed to a block of wood, a piece of a tree but now every tree is summoned to rejoice in the Lord.[5]

We come to God just as we are with our sin and our unbelief, and he gives us riches beyond compare and throws a Gospel party for us! Notice that:

- The call to repentance comes after the Lord's salvation already imparts to us. It is important to see our repentance does not save us. It is a response to the Lord delivering us from our blindness and our bondage to our idolatry. It says return to me because I have redeemed you. God's forgiveness of you is not dependent on your asking for it. Instead, you asking for it is dependent on him setting you free.

- There is reason for great joy. Is it any wonder that there is a call for great joy? God has done all the work, He gets all the glory. God will glorify himself through his people. We must beware of any formation of the Gospel that gives some of the glory to man. God will not share his glory with you.

Is that not incredible? Does that make you sing with wonder at the goodness of God? Does that make you want to return to him?

In fact, you don't want to completely forget your sins because you want to glory in God's forgiveness in them. To forget about them completely means you cannot remember and therefore glory in God's forgiveness of you. This is our testimony, not only our testimony of how we came to Christ, but of each and every day of his goodness.

We have two things on trial here. The first are the idols themselves. There they are. We've looked at them. They cannot deliver true happiness or joy, as much as we want them to.

God seals the deal on this by putting the proof in his own pudding. He says there will be a man named Cyrus who will deliver God's people. Cyrus will shepherd them, will fulfill his purpose, be God's anointed, and open doors before him. And over one hundred years later, that is exactly what happened. You can read about it in several Old Testament books, most notably at the end of 2 Chronicles and the beginning of Ezra.

This really happened. God did it. He is mighty to save. He even uses a pagan Persian king to accomplish his purposes lest anyone doubt in his sovereignty. That backdrop of the book is essential in understanding the veracity of God's claims.

God can predict the future because he controls it. That's how amazing he is. The other idols are just pretenders. Even Simon Cowell (the consummate cranky judge) has to admit there is only one winner. The others are all losers.

But we've also been on trial. The idols are exposed as false, but we're the ones who were worshiping them. What now for us?[6]

One answer is to wallow in our sins but then feel temporarily transformed by a saying like "God accepts you just as you are." However, this is not the biblical Gospel. The Gospel is better than unconditional love. God has contra-conditional love for you. Contra-conditional love says "God accepts you just as Christ is accepted."

Christ is fully pleasing to the Father, and he gives you his own perfect goodness. God never accepts me as-I-am; he accepts me as-I-am-in-Christ. The center of gravity is different. The true Gospel does not allow God's love to be sucked into the vortex of my soul's idolatrous systems. This psychological just-as-you-are approach soothes the unhappy soul without getting to the source of the pain.

In a moralizing approach, Christ's forgiveness is applied simply to behavioral sins. The solution is typically construed in all-or-nothing terms like, "Let go and let God," "repent for these behaviors," or "total yielded-ness" as an attempt to deal with the motive problems with a single act of housecleaning. There is little sense of patient process of inner renewal... daily dying to the false gods we fabricate.[7]

The Gospel is better than either of these, and it is available to you. Why?

God tells us: Even though you did not call upon me, O Christian, even though you have been weary of me, O Believer, even though you have not honored me or satisfied me, even though, in fact, if we're honest here, you have burdened me with your sins and you have wearied me with your iniquities.... Despite all that, God says, "I am he who blots out your transgressions for my own sake, and I will not remember your sins. Because you are my servant, whom I have chosen, and I am the Lord who made you, who formed you from the womb—because of this I will help you."

In Isaiah at the end of the 40s chapters and the beginning of the 50s, he calls over and over to his people. Listen! Awake! Watch! Hear!

Will you respond?

ISAIAH 53-54

We've come to one of the most famous passages in the Old Testament.

Portions of Isaiah 53 may be familiar to you. They were well-kmown verses to the writers of the New Testament because Isaiah is one of the most quoted books in the New Testament. I (Matt) was talking with a guy who is trying to read through the entire Bible, and he said when he gets bogged down in books like Numbers and Leviticus, he often turns to Isaiah 53 for a bit of reprieve since it points him to Jesus.

He then told me he recently read Isaiah 53 as he was going through the book, and it was a bit of a shock to read this chapter in its context. He is not the only person to struggle with understanding Isaiah. In Acts chapter 8, we encounter someone who has been reading through Isaiah, and he struggled to make sense of it too. What does Isaiah mean by what he wrote? Who is he talking about?

As we have studied Isaiah, we've asked over and over again, "What does it look like to be in the presence of greatness?" We've told stories of brushes with famous people. As we look at Isaiah 53, I want us to think about greatness again. What does it look like?

The Myth of Greatness

Is greatness Russell Westbrook breaking Oscar Robinson's triple double record? Is it Meb Keflezighi winning the Boston marathon? Simone Biles, Michael Phelps, Katie Ledecky, and Usain Bolt? In sports, it seems like there is always a debate about who is the greatest of all time (the GOAT).

Is it Alexander Graham Bell inventing the telephone? Is it getting straight As at school, graduating top of your class, or successfully defending your world-changing dissertation? Publishing your first book? Landing the job, the man, or the house?

What would you do to achieve greatness?

In 1989, a freshman named Alexi Santana arrived at Princeton University on a track scholarship. He could run the mile in just over four minutes. He was a short, narrow-framed, wiry guy with long hair who always wore a hat and walked hunched over. He was extremely shy. He was nice enough, but he didn't really make too many relationships during his time at Princeton. He excelled in the classroom. He seemed to effortlessly ace all of his exams, and he was a big track star.

According to his application, he was a cattle rancher from Nevada who was self-educated. He had slept under the stars for the past ten years. He read books he would get from the library when he was in town, and he liked to run in and around the desert of Nevada.

A few years later, a young woman named Renee who was studying at Yale came to a track meet and made eye contact with this guy she recognized named Jay Huntsman. Jay had gone to high school with her six years earlier in Palo Alto, California. The problem was that, according to a news report, Jay had died about three weeks after she had last seen him. She went and talked to the man, then to the coach, and then some people at Princeton.

Jay Huntsmen was actually Alexi Santana. And as the truth came out over the next day or two, his real name wasn't Alexi Santana. It was James Hogue. He was a convicted felon from Utah and who was thirty one years old. He had fabricated this identity and story based on what he perceived as the weaknesses of the admissions process at Princeton. He found out they liked people from Nevada, where they didn't have a lot of representation. They liked alternative, self-reliant stories, ones about someone who was self-educated. According to his application, both of his parents were dead, and he had accomplished all this on his own. He used this story to get into Princeton because he was convinced the way to get ahead and achieve greatness in life was to get a degree from an Ivy League school[1]

You may not have done anything as dramatic or illegal as James Hogue. But we can relate to this desire to do whatever it takes to achieve greatness. We want to matter, to be great. Our life works around this desire to achieve greatness. We customize our behavior depending on who we are around so people will like us, so our relationships are successful, or so we can build a certain kind of reputation.

We think greatness is found in getting ahead in our jobs. We prioritize our careers instead of loving our families or taking care of ourselves. We view money as a sign of greatness. The number of zeros in your bank account or how our portfolio is doing matters most. We want to make a name for ourselves.

We believe we will achieve greatness if we are able to do the most deadlifts, qualify for the Boston marathon, be the homecoming queen, graduate top of the class, or buy that new car or bigger house. Snag that deal. Win the competition. Outsmart the others.

This myth of greatness shapes much of North American culture, and so does the core value of rugged individualism and pulling yourself up by your own bootstraps. It is the story of humanity.

Think back with me to the book of Genesis. God created Adam and Eve, and they lived in a garden paradise. They had it all. They were God's vicegerent and representatives, and they were to exercise authority over all creation.

They had greatness. They were living in perfect relationship with God as he had created them to be.

But the serpent slithers in and begins to tell lies about what it means to be great. The snake tells them that they don't need God to inform their lives: "God can't tell you what to do. Why would God tell you not to eat of the tree of knowledge of good and evil? Does he really have your best interest in mind? God is holding back on you!"

Adam and Eve believed they could forge their own way. By eating of the tree of knowledge of good and evil, they would achieve greatness on their own terms. They saw the tree was good for food and was a delight to the eyes. It would make them wise. They rested in themselves and their achievement to find greatness.

Instead of bringing greatness, this sin brought brokenness and alienation. This story shapes humanity. It is the myth of greatness. We believe greatness is found in ourselves. Isaiah 53:6 diagnoses our condition perfectly: *"All we like sheep have gone astray; we have turned every one to his own way."*

We have turned to our own way, thinking we can achieve greatness on our own.

Unexpected Greatness

The story of Adam and Eve is what makes Isaiah 53 unexpected. This is the fourth of the Servant Songs in Isaiah.

The northern tribe of Israel has been taken into captivity by Assyria, and they are scattered into the nations. The southern tribe of Judah will be carried into captivity by Babylon. God's people have turned to their own way. Like we do, they sought greatness in themselves.

But God has promised his Servant will be the one to bring deliverance.

That is what the rest of Isaiah is about—God's promised redemption. Isaiah 42 says God will put his Spirit on his Servant, and he will bring justice to the nations. In chapter 44, we read that God will bless the Servant with many descendants. In chapter 49, we read his ministry will be effective in word and deed. He will gather his people to himself, and he will be a light for the nations. In chapter 50, we realize the servant will be obedient to the Lord. This will be a leader of Israel unlike any other seen before, one of true greatness. We are expecting a great, powerful, mighty leader.

Perhaps unexpectedly, we read that everyone will be repulsed by this servant. Look at Isaiah 53:3: *"He was despised and rejected by men, a man of sorrows and acquainted with grief."* Verse 4 says, *"He has borne our griefs and carried our sorrows."*

I would have thought the Great Redeemer would be heralded

above all others, radiant and spectacular. He's going to be despised and rejected by men?

Wait—this is greatness?

Yes, this is greatness, and this is the story of the Bible. In his greatness, God enters into brokenness. When Adam and Eve rejected God and chose to find greatness in themselves, God pursued them. He entered into their brokenness to pursue reconciliation. He even comes in brokenness.

God defines what greatness is. It is entering into the brokenness of the world. That is why this is such an unexpected passage, and it's why greatness is so surprising.

God enters into suffering to bring *shalom*—forgiveness and wholeness. In Genesis 3, after Adam and Eve rebel, God enters into their suffering to bring salvation.

Think about the people living in slavery in Egypt at the beginning of Exodus. God enters into their suffering to save them. If you read the Old Testament, over and over again you see God's people in suffering, and God enters into that situation to bring salvation.

Look at 53:2. What type of soil does this servant grow up in?—dry ground. You don't plant a seed in dry ground. But God did. He planted a seed, there and his son took root in the unlikeliest of conditions. This is where God roots himself. Verses 2–3 tell us he walked in the contempt of people. This is how the long-awaited servant of God lived. Nobody thought he was beautiful. No one was interested in what he had to say. Verse 4 tells us he knew grief, and he carried our sorrows. Verses 7–8 tell us he forsook his deserved self-defense. He was afflicted and accused, and yet he did not open his mouth.

Why does he do all this? Why does the servant undergo such suffering? In 53:10, we read it was the will of God to crush him.

Whoa, that sounds crazy. The servant is going to be crushed by God? Why?

He is crushed because of love. This entire passage points us to Jesus, the Savior who was born into a broken world.

For God so loved the world that what? He sent his son, Jesus. It is this Jesus who entered into a broken and suffering world. It is this Jesus who grew up out of dry ground. He grew up in the contempt of others, carried our grief and sorrows, and he loves us.

Isaiah 53 points us to a Great Savior who enters into our brokenness, was wounded for our transgressions, and crushed for our
iniquities.

This is greatness, and it is the good news of the Gospel. We have
a Savior who entered into our world of waywardness and sin. A
Savior who actually lived the life you should live. He lived a life of
greatness, a life that truly loved God and loved his neighbor as
himself. He lived the perfect, righteous life, one of greatness. He
loves the sheep who have gone astray.

The Gospel tells us greatness is found in a Suffering who gave his
life as an offering for sin. This Servant came to live a life of suffering
and rejection, one filled with love for wayward sheep. As a shepherd,
he gave his life and bore the sin of his sheep.

This is the greatness of the Gospel. It is an unexpected greatness,
but it is what we need. God demonstrates his love for us in that
while we were still sinners, Christ died for us. He did not wait for us
to get our act together or to come to him. No. Out of love, God
entered into our brokenness.

Mission of Greatness

Isaiah 53 is an unexpected passage, but it is such a great one! I hope
this story of greatness shapes your life. Because if it is the story that
shapes your life, it will change everything. You will not be able to
contain it.

It will lead you into greatness and then into rejoicing.

God does not just enter into suffering just because he loves a
tough challenge. He does it to bring redemption. God does not plant
a root into dry ground to watch it wither and die. Miraculously, that
root planted in dry ground grows, and it brings salvation. In Isaiah,
we see that greatness enters into brokenness and brings salvation.
That changes everything, and it sends us out on an amazing mission.
As we enter into suffering and brokenness, there is an expectation of
redemption. There is expectation that a root out of dry ground will
grow!

Isaiah 54 says:

Sing O barren one, who did not bear; break forth into singing and cry aloud you who have not been in labor! For the children of the desolate one will be more than the children of her who is married," Says the LORD. "Enlarge the place of your tent and let the curtains of your habitations be stretched out; do not hold back; lengthen your cords and strengthen your stakes. For you will be spread abroad to the right and to the left, and your offspring will possess the nations and will people the desolate cities. (Isa. 54:1-3)

What does this mean for us? We learn that there is hope, and we can enter into brokenness and suffering. God has entered into our glorious, fallen world, and, as a result of the good news of the Gospel, we can enter into the suffering and brokenness of the world. This is the mission of greatness.

I have friends who travel to India every year to work with what are called "the untouchables." These are the lowest of the low in the caste system. They are the poorest of the poor. People don't acknowledge them or touch them.

My friends tell me that just to physically touch and pray for these people shows them Jesus. There is strong opposition to the Gospel in India, but the church continues to grow. Many women who come to faith in Jesus are beaten and put out of their homes. Yet the church continues to grow. One pastor used to bang a drum as he entered a village to teach about Jesus. The villagers told him they would hit him for every time he beat that drum, and they proceeded to do just that.

One pastor was in his eighties, and as he entered a village to proclaim the greatness of the Gospel, he was beaten so severely he was hospitalized for three months. After he got out of the hospital, he went straight back to the village where he was assaulted.

The villagers asked, "Why are you here?" He said, "I have to tell you about Jesus."

This is greatness—finding life in our Suffering Servant and telling others about him.

ISAIAH 55

For Isaiah 55, I want you to think of the best meal you have ever eaten. Is it steak tartare while in the south of France, tacos in Central America, or that home cooked goodness only Grandma can make? Is it sea bass at Waterbar in San Francisco, perfectly cooked steak at Flemings in Utica Square, or duck and risotto in Scotland? Is it the filet at Boulevard which melts like butter paired with a Rombauer cabernet? Or BBQ while being filmed for *The Great Food Truck Race?*

If Kraft macaroni and cheese or chicken nuggets is your idea of great food, trust me, there is something so much better out there.

I have a friend who knows where all the best restaurants are. Amy and I (Matt) love going to dinner with him and his wife because we know it's going to be a great meal with great friends.

One of his favorite spots to eat is the Signature Grill in Edmond. He loves the food there and has gotten to know the chef well. Every time he goes to eat there, he tells the staff to have Clay (the chef) make him dinner. He doesn't order anything off the menu. He just says whatever amazing feast Clay wants to create—let him work his magic. Clay has made him some of the greatest meals he has ever eaten. He will often send me a picture of a beautiful plate Clay has created—they make my mouth water—then he describes the meal to me. "I had a steak and shrimp with the most amazing seasoning I ever had, and mushrooms stuffed with asparagus, and an exotic cheese."

This passage in Isaiah 55 describes an amazing meal. It is an invitation to the greatest feast you can possibly imagine.

In the last chapter as we looked at Isaiah 53–54, we saw God had promised to send a Savior—his Servant—to deliver his people in exile. There was anticipation of a powerful and great savior. But as Isaiah 53 unfolded, we saw God's Savior was a Suffering Servant. He entered into our suffering and brokenness, and he took all of it onto himself. He took the iniquity of us all, and by his wounds we are healed. This suffering servant brings salvation. Our sins are forgiven, and we are reconciled to God.

In chapter 54, we noted this salvation goes out into all the world. It is bigger than we could possibly imagine. Today as we look at chapter 55, we see an invitation to enter the feast and celebration of this great salvation. As we look at the passage we will look at two things: the invitation to the feast and extending the invitation.

The Invitation to the Feast

We serve a God who pursues his people. That is the story of the Bible.

We serve a God who is welcoming us as the great inviter. That is what this passage is about.

He has prepared a feast, a banquet. He is throwing a party, and he invites people to come and join in.

Come to the party! Isaiah writes:

Come, everyone who thirsts, come to the waters; and he who has no money, come, buy and eat! Come, buy wine and milk without money and without price. (Isa. 55:1)

One commentator said it is like a street vendor selling his goods or the popcorn guy at the baseball game.[1] But it is so much better than that. He's not selling $9 beer or $10 cotton candy.

This is the call of God to come into his kingdom to find restoration and healing. This text is an invitation into the salvation of the servant to enjoy this great feast.

The feast is the picture of the Kingdom of God, a metaphor or a picture of heaven. Heaven is described in many ways in the Bible, but the most consistent image of life with God in his kingdom is a party, a feast, a banquet.

This feast is one of abundance and grace:

Come, everyone who thirsts, come to the waters; and he who has no money, come, buy and eat! Come, buy wine and milk without money and without price. (Isa. 55:1)

Water is a life-giving sustenance that quenches your thirst.

We all know what it is like to be thirsty. Amy and I like to run, and when it's really hot, ice-cold water tastes especially good.

But God's feast does not just have water. It has wine and milk. It is nourishing and joyful. God is calling his people to come find restoration, nourishment, and joy.

It is a feast of life. Verse 3 says, *"Incline your ear, come to me; hear that your soul may live and I will make with you an everlasting covenant."* This feast is about coming to God. It is an invitation to life with God. The feast is God himself and being connected to God. It is life for your soul.

That is good news, and here is the best part—you are invited. It's for everyone who thirsts, for anyone who has need.

That's you.

In the context of Isaiah, God sends an invitation to his people who are in exile in Babylon. He says, "I will save you. I will deliver you. You are invited to my feast."

The problem is an alternative, seductive feast. Babylon is offering a dinner as well. It promotes a life apart from God, making promises of prosperity and life.

Many of God's people are looking for life in Babylon. They don't consider themselves in exile anymore. They think they have found it exactly where they want to be. They are working hard to make a life for themselves in exile, and they are comfortable feasting on Babylon's delicacies. They believe the lie of the snake in the Garden that says you can do life without God.

God urges them not to believe the lies of the serpent and not to try and find life in Babylon. Verse 2 says:

Why do you spend your money for that which is not bread and your labor for that which does not satisfy? Listen diligently to me, and eat what is good, and delight yourselves in rich food.

What about you? Where are you looking for life? What are you chasing after to give you life? What are you searching for? What are you experimenting with and looking for to satisfy your soul?

Oftentimes we switch out what we have for something better, newer, or faster. We get a different car, house, wife, a new computer, boat, phone, season tickets, grill, diet, haircut—all in the hopes of finding the thing that really satisfies. The reality is just what the Rolling Stones sing—we can't get no satisfaction, and we try, try, and try. We labor for that which does not satisfy.

It is like the Nathan's Hot Dog eating contest, that great American feast celebrated every Fourth of July. I remember when Takeru Kobayashi was dominant in this event, and when Joey Chestnut took him out. Now there are guys gunning for Joey Chestnut. This year, I got the kids all excited about this event. We couldn't wait to watch the Nathan's Hot Dog eating contest—who needs fireworks? Then the event started, and they witnessed guys shoving hot dogs in their mouths, dipping buns in water, and continually stuffing their faces.

My kids were not entertained. They were disgusted. They asked, "Why would anyone do that?" And said, "I don't ever want to eat a hot dog again!"

That is what we do. We gorge ourselves on something like fifty hot dogs and think it will give us life. We give ourselves to anything and everything but God, and we think it will give us life and joy. We labor for that which does not satisfy.

But the good news is that God enters in. He pursues us and invites us to his banquet. He calls us to listen diligently to him. He invites us to delight in rich food.

Jesus tells a parable in Luke 14 that describes this:

A man once gave a great banquet and invited many. And at the time for the banquet he sent his servant to say to those who had been invited, "Come, for everything is now ready." But they all alike began to make excuses. The first said to him, "I have bought a field, and I must go out and see it. Please have me excused." And another said, "I have bought five yoke of oxen, and I go to examine them. Please have me excused." And another said, "I have married a wife, and therefore I cannot come." So the servant came and reported these things to his master. Then the master of the house became angry and said to his servant, "Go out quickly to the streets and lanes of the city, and bring in the poor and crippled and blind and lame." And the servant said, "Sir, what you commanded has been done, and still there is room." And the master said to the servant, "Go out to the highways and hedges and compel people to come in, that my house may be filled. For I tell you, none of those men who were invited shall taste my banquet." (Luke 14:16–24)

God seeks out his people and invites them to this great banquet. I am sobered by this passage and the propensity we have to try and live without God. We are able to come up with all types of excuses to refuse the invitation of God. That is why there is an urgency to respond to this invitation. We see this in 55:6–8:

Seek the LORD while he may be found call upon him while he is near; let the wicked forsake his way, and the unrighteous man his thoughts; let him return to the LORD, that he may have compassion on him and to our God, for he will abundantly pardon. For my thoughts are not your thoughts, neither are your ways my ways, declares the LORD.

The invitation of God might go this way:

I am here to deliver you from your sin. Stop eating nasty hot dogs. That is gross. Let's ask Chef Cody to make you a meal you'll never forget. Come to me. I am here to deliver you. I will teach you to walk in new ways, ways that are not your ways, and I will give you new thoughts, thoughts that are not your thoughts. I am going to draw you out of this sin holding you in bondage.

This is beautiful. God promises to deliver his people, the ones who have forsaken him and seek life in Babylon. Yet, he promises to deliver them and put them on a new path. There is abundant pardon with God.

This is the good news of the Gospel. God knows our need better than we do, and he sent Jesus to be our savior. Jesus is the one who came into this world. He entered into our brokenness and lived the perfect life for us. He lived a life without sin, and he went to the cross for his wayward sheep. He went to the cross for those who gorge on hot dogs.[2]

I was talking with a pastor about this passage, and he said this reminded him of Luke 15 and the parable of the prodigal son. The prodigal son rejected his father and sought life on his own. When that didn't work out, the son found himself desperately needy and hungry. He ended up with a job feeding pigs and was so hungry, he longed for the food pigs eat. In the son's desperation, he came to himself and returned to his father's home.

Yes that is true, but that is not the whole story. The prodigal did reject his father and sought to do life on his own. In fact, he spent everything he had on things that didn't satisfy. He realized his need and decided to go back home, but he wanted to go back and work as a hired servant. He wanted to go home and try and earn his way back into his father's house.

But out of love and compassion, the father rushes out to meet his son. The son can't even relay his plan to work for his dad because his dad is too busy embracing him and kissing him and celebrating. The son is welcomed home. He will not be a servant. The best robe is put on him, he is given a ring and shoes, and they throw a big party. The fattened calf is killed.

We serve a God who loves us and pursues us even when we seek him with wrong motives.

This is the beauty of the Gospel. The reality is all you need to come to the feast is need.

One of our hymns is "Come Ye Sinners." It says all you need is to feel your need of him. All you need is need. What do you need to come into the feast? Need! Do you see your need this morning? Do you see your brokenness? Do you see your need for a savior?

The good news is we have a Savior. God demonstrates his love for us in that while we were still sinners—while we were still eating all those hot dogs—Christ died for us.

And what did Jesus say on the cross?—*tetelestai*—it is finished! It is bought and paid for. Your invitation to the feast is bought and paid for by the life, death, and resurrection of Jesus Christ. That is good news! This is the invitation to the feast: *"Come everyone who thirsts, come to the waters, and he who has no money, come buy and eat!"* (Isa. 55:1).

Extending the Invitation

When you receive this invitation to the feast, you become inviters to it too. You extend the appeal to others. In 55:3–4, God has made a covenant with David, showing his steadfast love. This should be somewhat surprising to find in the book of Isaiah, which comes a long time after when David lived. But David stands as a witness to the love of God and then in verse 5, there is a call to be a witness to the nations. A witness is like being a reporter telling everyone what he or she has seen and experienced.

Everyone who has encountered God and been invited to the feast is then propelled out into the world in mission. This is the experience of many in the Bible—like Isaiah. Remember in chapter 6 when he encountered a holy God? He saw his sin, experienced the purification of sin, and then was sent out on mission.

The same is true for us. We are sent into the world to be a witness. The church is to be an inviting, hospitable, and welcoming culture. That is who we are as Christ-followers. We are sent to invite others to the feast. We are to be a people who care deeply about those who are not at the party.

That is why Christians should throw great parties. We want to invite others to the feast, to come and meet Jesus.

Are you willing to become an inviter? Are you inviting people into your homes? To parties, your small group, and your church? Christianity is meant to be an inviting culture where we keep on declaring "Come taste and see that the Lord is good."

Unfortunately, oftentimes we aren't good inviters because we forget the Gospel. We forget our own call to the feast and that the Gospel is good news.

The good news is that God's word still goes out. We can have hope in it. It is true and trustworthy. The Kingdom of God has come, and it is coming. We read:

For as the rain and the snow come down from heaven and do not return there but water the earth, making it bring forth and sprout, giving seed to the sower and bread to the eater, so shall my word be that goes out from my mouth; it shall not return to me empty, but it shall accomplish that which I purpose, and shall succeed in the thing for which I sent it. (Isa. 55:10–11)

This is good news. It is good news we can take comfort in, and that we can share with others:

For you shall go out in joy and be led forth in peace the mountains and the hills before you shall break forth into singing, and all the trees of the field shall clap their hands. Instead of the thorn shall come up the cypress; instead of the brier shall come up the myrtle; and it shall make a name for the Lord, an everlasting sign that shall not be cut off. (Isa. 55:12–13)

This is a beautiful picture of hope and shalom. Think about this in its context of a people in exile. It's a promise of a homecoming and of freedom. Imagine the hope it would bring.

God created all things good. There was shalom, but we decided we could live apart from God. Humanity feasted on rebellion as we ate of the tree of knowledge of good and evil. Thorns and thistles—sin and separation—entered the world, but God pursued us. He said, "I will make all things right." This is the story of the Bible.

Through Jesus' life, death, and resurrection, your sins are forgiven, and all things will be made right. Peace has come. You have a place at the table. All things will be made new.

That is our hope. Because of this, we welcome others to the feast, and there is plenty of room here! We must remember this good news and our story of rescue.

God is sending you into mission. There are hands that only you can hold. There are hearts breaking that only you can mend. God has uniquely put things in your story where you can love someone in a way others can't. God is sending you out to call others to come!

So I invite you now: *"Come, everyone who thirsts, come to the waters; and he who has no money, come, buy and eat! Come, buy wine and milk without money and without price"* (Isa. 55:1).

ISAIAH 58, 61, 62

What is something you thought would be terrible but turned out great? What is a food you thought would be awful, but then you tried it and found out it was delicious?

I (Matt) have a friend who always thought she would hate sushi. It just sounded gross. Raw fish—who would eat raw fish? Then she tried it, and it became her favorite food.

What about people you thought might be bad?

Do you remember Susan Boyle?[1] She appeared on "Britain's Got Talent" years ago. When she first appeared for her audition, there was nothing about her appearance to make you think this would be a great performance. The audience and judges were cynical about how the audition would go.

Then she opened her mouth and shocked everyone when she sang "I Dreamed a Dream" from *Les Misérables*. Nobody expected such a great voice or a great singer.

We have also seen some examples of unexpected greatness in Isaiah. In the chapters leading up to Isaiah 53, the case is being made for a leader of Israel unlike any other seen before, a leader of true greatness. We are expecting a great leader, a powerful, mighty one who will deliver the people from exile.

But in Isaiah 53:3 we read something unexpected: *"He was despised and rejected by men, a man of sorrows and acquainted with grief."* He entered into and took our suffering and brokenness. He took the iniquity of us all, and by his wounds we are healed. This suffering servant brings salvation. Our sins are forgiven, and we are reconciled to God. It is an unexpected great salvation. In chapter 54, we see this salvation goes out into all the world, and it is bigger than we could possibly imagine. In chapter 55, we saw the people were invited to an amazing feast: *"Come, everyone who thirsts, come to the waters; and he who has no money, come, buy and eat! Come, buy wine and milk without money and without price"* (Isa. 55:1).

In the passages we read in 58–62, we see some unexpected things as well. I want to look at them under three headings: unexpected worship, unexpected salvation, and unexpected mission.

Unexpected Worship

God's people have been delivered from exile. Many have returned to rebuild the ruins of Jerusalem and the temple and to reestablish the worship of God. They are to live as God's people and as his kingdom representatives. They are called to live as people who have been loved by God and therefore love God and others, to be a blessing to the world.

If you take a cursory glance at Isaiah 58, it looks like the people are serious about following God, especially in worship:

> *Yet they seek me daily and delight to know my ways, as if they were a nation that did righteousness and did not forsake the judgment of their God; they ask of me righteous judgments; they delight to draw near to God.* (Isa. 58:2)

Every day, they are seeking out the Lord in worship. They are fasting, and that is pretty dedicated. They seem to be eager to know God's ways. They delight in drawing near to God. These are good God-fearing folk, right? They pray, read their Bibles, fast, and they do all this diligently.

In 58:1, we read the prophet is to *"Cry aloud; do not hold back; lift up your like a trumpet; declare to my people their transgression, to the house of Jacob their sins."* Lift up your voice like a trumpet—make noise, holler, and shout it from the mountain tops. What is he to cry out? What is he to shout out like a trumpet? He is pointing out the people's transgression and their sin.

Wait, what sin? They seem to be diligent and passionate about their worship. What is their sin? The people ask this question: "What are we doing wrong God? We are worshiping you, so why are you not responding?" Look at verse 3: *"Why have we fasted, and you see it not? Why have we humbled ourselves, and you take no knowledge of it?"*

So how does God answer? In verses 3–4, he says:

> *Behold, in the day of your fast you seek your own pleasure, and oppress all your workers. Behold, you fast only to quarrel and to fight and to hit with a wicked fist. Fasting like yours this day will not make your voice to be heard on high.*

In essence, God is saying:

> Yes you do a lot of external things like fasting, but this is not the kind of fast I am looking for. You do a ton of religious activities, but at the same time you oppress your workers. You get together for worship but spend all your time fighting.

They have divorced their love for God from their love for their neighbor. They have separated their love for God from their love for others, and it messes everything up.

We are guilty of this too.

We love to compartmentalize our lives. We treat Christianity like a formalized ritual. We believe if we show up for church on Sunday and do all the activities, then we are good for the week. Or we treat Christianity like a purely intellectual exercise.

Many of us love our doctrine, but we make it mostly intellectual. Or we treat Christianity like a private decision we make, but it doesn't impact any other portion of our lives or the way we relate to others.

We also make worship a means to get what we want. We seek to manipulate God, thinking, "If I do all these good things, then God will bless me." We treat God as someone we can appease through worship. We believe if we perform these rituals, we will earn the favor of God. We are treating God just like the pagan gods of the Babylonian or Persian empire.

God says:

This is not what it looks like to worship me. This is not what it looks like to be in relationship with me. This is not what it looks like to be my people.

We see the worship God wants in verses 6–7:

Is not this the fast that I choose: to loose the bonds of wickedness, to undo the straps of the yoke, to let the oppressed go free, and break every yoke? Is it not to share your bread with the hungry and bring the homeless poor into your house; when you see the naked to cover him, and not to hide yourself from your own flesh.

You cannot have a meaningful relationship with God and not be deeply concerned for people. God is saying, "These are the spiritual disciplines I want. This is the kind of worship I want. It is to care for the oppressed, to feed the hungry, and to clothe the poor."

This not just God speaking in Isaiah. It is all over the scriptures. In James 1:27, we read, *"Religion that is pure and undefiled before God the Father is this: to visit orphans and widows in their affliction and to keep oneself unstained from the world."* True religion is moving toward people in pain and people in need.

We see this also at very beginning of Isaiah in chapter 1. God criticizes their worship and calls their rituals an abomination (1:13). Then in verse 17 he says, *"Seek justice, correct oppression; bring justice to the fatherless, plead the widow's cause."* You can't separate loving God from loving others.

In Proverbs 14:31, we read, *"Whoever oppresses a poor man insults his Maker, but he who is generous to the needy honors him."* Proverbs 19:17 says, *"Whoever is generous to the poor lends to the Lord."*

Do you see this love for God and love for people? You can't separate them.

Matthew 25 is another example. Jesus is talking about the final judgment and how the people will be separated into sheep and goats. Listen to verses 41–45:

> Then he will say to those on his left, "Depart from me, you cursed, into the eternal fire prepared for the devil and his angels. For I was hungry and you gave me no food, I was thirsty and you gave me no drink, I was a stranger and you did not welcome me, naked and you did not clothe me, sick and in prison and you did not visit me." Then they also will answer, saying, "Lord, when did we see you hungry or thirsty or a stranger or naked or sick or in prison, and did not minister to you?" Then he will answer them, saying, "Truly, I say to you, as you did not do it to one of the least of these, you did not do it to me."

Jesus is saying, "If you don't love the poor, hungry, vulnerable, and the needy, then you don't love me." Is that how you think of worship? I don't know about you, but it is not the way I often view worship. It certainly was not the way the people of Judah considered it.

This is an unexpected worship.

So what do we do? Is the solution to just go out and love the poor, hungry, and the vulnerable? Should we just try harder and do better?

That won't work.

My wife, Amy, was at a meeting about community renewal, and the speaker said that if we are going to see change in our community and love for our neighbors, we need to appeal to the goodness in humanity to go out and accomplish this.

That won't work because as a result of sin in the world, we know there is no one good, no one righteous, no one who seeks God (Rom. 3:10). When Adam and Eve sinned in the garden, it did not just bring separation in their relationship with God, but it also brought separation in their relationship with one another. They could not love God. They could not love their neighbor as themselves. They needed a savior. So do we. And the good news is God has sent a savior—and he brings an unexpected salvation.

Unexpected Salvation

In Isaiah 61, we read about a savior who is coming who has the anointing of the Lord. He is sent to bring good news to the poor, and he will proclaim the Lord's favor.

We know this points us forward to Jesus. When Jesus began his public ministry in Luke 4, he went into the synagogue and read from Isaiah 61. He read:

> *The Spirit of the Lord is upon me, because he has anointed me to proclaim good news to the poor. He has sent me to proclaim liberty to the captives and recovering of sight to the blind, to set at liberty those who are oppressed, to proclaim the year of the Lord's favor.* (Luke 4:18–19)

Then, giving the scroll back to the attendant and with all eyes on him, he told them, *"Today this has been fulfilled in your hearing"* (Luke 4:21).

Now what does Jesus mean in this verse? Some would say this is all spiritual metaphors that Jesus is applying to these words from Isaiah. Jesus did not come to meet our physical needs but only our spiritual ones. Others would say Jesus came only to meet physical needs, and he came to bring social justice.

Here is the good news—Jesus came for both the spiritually poor and the materially poor. Jesus spent a ton of time with the outcasts, with the poor and needy. It is all over the New Testament. We see Jesus feeding and healing and treating people with dignity.

He also died on the cross and took the punishment for our sins. We have forgiveness of sins because of Christ's atoning work on the cross. Jesus comes for the spiritually, economically, psychologically, and the socially poor. Jesus comes for broken and needy people.

The Second International Congress on World Evangelization was held in 1989 (the first was held in 1974, also known as the Lausanne Conference). It produced a statement summarizing beliefs on evangelism. Here is some of what it says:

> The gospel comes as good news to both. The spiritually poor, who,
> whatever their economic circumstances, humble themselves before

God, receive by faith the free gift of salvation. There is no other way for anybody to enter the kingdom of God. The materially poor and powerless find in addition a new dignity as God's children, and the love of brothers and sisters who will struggle with them for their liberation from everything which demeans or oppresses them.[2]

Jesus's ministry has to be spiritual. What does it mean when Jesus said he has come to proclaim liberty to the captives? What captives did he release from prison? How many people were freed from prison? Certainly not John the Baptist. He was killed in jail.

But think about that phrase in spiritual terms. How many spiritual captives were set free from the bondage of sin and self-centeredness by the life death and resurrection of Jesus? There has to be this type of dimension to the ministry of Jesus.

Also, Jesus' ministry has to have social and economic dimensions. Jesus spent much of his time with the poor. He welcomed the unclean and the outcast.

In 61:2, we read he has come *"to proclaim the year of the LORD's favor."* This is a reference to the Old Testament and the Year of Jubilee. It was easy to fall into debt in the Old Testament, just like it is today. People were trapped in a cycle of debt they couldn't escape.

The good news was that every seven years was a Sabbath. That meant debts were forgiven and servants were freed. But every seven Sabbaths, after forty nine years, on the fiftieth year, the Year of Jubilee took place. If your family had lost property due to famine and debt, it had to be returned in the Year of Jubilee. There was forgiveness and restoration.

Jesus says his ministry is like a Jubilee. The kingdom he brings will be one of forgiveness and restoration., the righting of wrongs, the wiping away of tears, and the undoing of inequalities.

The Gospel has spiritual, social, and economic significance. It encompasses everything. Jesus said, *"Today, this scripture has been fulfilled in your hearing"* (Luke 4:21). Jesus announces that the Kingdom of God has come. Jesus is the anointed one of God. He is the Messiah, the one sent to bring the Kingdom of God.

Jesus is an unexpected Messiah, and he brings an unexpected

salvation. After he makes this proclamation in Luke 4, the people began to grumble. He is not what they were expecting. He is the son of Joseph, so how can he be a great prophet?

Then Jesus begins to tell them how the Kingdom of God is not just for the Jewish people but for Gentiles too. That made them so angry that they tried to kill him by throwing him off a cliff.

Much of Jesus' ministry created controversy. People didn't like the type of people he associated with. He ate with sinners and outcasts. No self-respecting Jewish person would eat with anyone who would make him or her religiously unclean. They didn't like Jesus' social agenda because it did not match theirs. They were deeply concerned with social policy. They were looking for a messiah who would meet their social needs, one who would throw off the yoke of Roman oppression. When Jesus did not meet their messianic expectations, they had him killed.

The good news is that while Jesus may not have been the messiah we expected, he is the one we need. He lived the perfect life for you. He lived a life of love, worship, and devotion to God. He lived a life of love for others, one of love for the poor, needy, and outcast.

He also went to the cross for you, taking your brokenness and shame. He was forsaken so you could be accepted. He lived the life we should have lived but don't, and he died the death we deserve to die. He rose again to make all things new.

In Isaiah 61:3, we read the Messiah has come:

> To grant them a beautiful head-dress instead of ashes, the oil of gladness instead of mourning, the garment of praise instead of a faint spirit, that they may be called oaks of righteousness, the planting of the LORD, that he may be glorified.

Jesus has come to take away the shame and brokenness of the Fall. He has come to take away the mourning, ashes, and brokenness of this world. The wages of sin is ashes, but Jesus came to give beauty instead of ashes. He has come to make all things new—to put back together that which sin has ripped apart. His life, death, and resurrection brings restoration. It restores our relationship with God. We are given a beautiful headdress and the oil of gladness.

In Isaiah 62, we see we are given a righteousness. We are given a new name, and we are called *"My Delight Is in Her"* (Isa. 62:4). God delights in you! He loves you. He loves you so much he sent Jesus to bring reconciliation and restoration. We read: *"As the bridegroom rejoices over his bride, so shall your God rejoice over you"* (Isa. 62:5). God rejoices over you. Do you believe that?

This is the good news of the Gospel. Because of the finished work of Christ, your sins are forgiven, your shame is taken away, and your dignity is restored. You have his righteousness. God takes delight in you, and he rejoices over you.

Hallelujah—what a Savior!

Hallelujah—what an unexpected salvation!

Unexpected Mission

We not only have restoration as a result of the Gospel, but we have a mission. We are sent out. Those who have been renewed by the Gospel and have been healed in Christ—are sent out. We're made beautiful by Jesus, and we have a new name and relationship.

We can't stay in. We have to be on the move.

Look at what Isaiah 61:4 says:

> They shall build up the ancient ruins; they shall raise up the former devastations;
> they shall repair the ruined cities, the devastations of many generations.

Do you hear the mission? We are to go and rebuild cities. We are not afraid of the city or the problems of the world. We enter in and move toward pain and brokenness—not away from it.

Because of the Gospel, we can enter in. We have become healed healers, and saved servants. Jesus has brought the Kingdom of God, and we are to be about the work of the kingdom. We live lives that display the value of the kingdom which means better schools, neighborhoods, and communities.

I met a lady who raises money for a back-to-school bash that provides school supplies for needy kids in Shawnee. I asked her how she got involved, and she told me that a few years ago she was homeless and lost custody of her kids. A local church found her a place to live with someone. The church had resources that could help people get a job or job training.

As they began to care for her, she did not understand why someone would take an interest in her. She said she had too many problems and couldn't be helped. The lady she was staying with said, "Anne, you don't have too many problems. We are helping you because we love you."

Anne protested and said, "You can't love me."

The lady said, "Anne, I can and do love you because of Jesus and his love for me." Anne did not feel that Jesus could possibly love her. She wasn't good enough to deserve his love. She didn't think Jesus would have anything to do with her. She had long ago quit believing in a god who would let her live in such turmoil and pain.

This lady began reading the stories of Jesus with Anne. She was showing her that Jesus knew what it was like to be poor and even homeless. She read stories about how Jesus cared about women, ones who had been abused by men and were outcast in society. She saw how Jesus loved them, spent time with them, and entered into their brokenness.

Jesus offered a woman water that would truly satisfy her thirst. Anne saw Jesus had compassion on a woman who had suffered physically for years, and the health care system had drained her of all her resources. Jesus brought healing. Anne saw Jesus knew what it meant to be arrested and abused by the police.

She said:

Jesus knows what it means to be me. He knows my physical, psychological, social, economic, and spiritual needs. I began to see Jesus and his love in this lady who was caring for me. We were reading the Bible together, but I was seeing her live this life of love, and it was overwhelming, and it changed my life.

This is why Anne is going around town raising money from businesses in Shawnee to make sure kids have school supplies for the upcoming school year. This is why the core group of Shawnee Pres is a part of this back-to-school bash.

Why? Because this is what it means to be a follower of Jesus. As those who have been clothed by the love of Jesus, who have been clothed in his righteousness, who know the Lord takes delight in you and rejoices over you, who know what it means to be liberated—our mission is to go and proclaim the year of the Lord's favor.

ISAIAH 63-66

Here in our last chapters of Isaiah, I (Doug) want to ask for you to think of a place that's wonderful, somewhere that takes your breath away.

Maybe it's Busch Stadium, a lake house, a castle, or a cathedral. Or Owen Field or Boone Pickens Stadium on a brisk Saturday afternoon with Game Day in town. The top of a mountain ridge, the beach, lake, or your favorite river. Perhaps it's a sailing trip, skiing, or the last few days of your honeymoon.

Here in Oklahoma (a tourist hotspot!), you might really enjoy the Science Museum, the Botanical Gardens, or the zoo. You might want to visit the Art Museum, the Land Run Monument, the Cowboy Hall of Fame, the Banjo Hall of Fame, or the Carrier Pigeon Hall of Fame. You might go out to the Wichitas, the Great Salt Plains, or head over to the Philbrook Museum of Art in Tulsa.

Or you might dream of Paris, Iceland, the Fiji Islands, Disneyland, Legoland, a good friend's front porch, or a quiet night in your own house with everything clean and put away....

Where do you want to be?

It's always a bittersweet feeling to get to the end of the book we've been studying. We've been looking at, thinking about, and discussing Isaiah, and soon we will be finished. He has challenged us with our sin, idolatry, and our too-low conception of God. He has pushed our view of what God can do in history and creation. He has set before us the idea of a Suffering Servant who will come as a conquering king and yet come in humiliation in order to take our sins on himself. He has set all this in the context of the Ancient Near East, telling stories of Ahaz, Hezekiah, Sennacherib, and Cyrus—two Jewish kings, an Assyrian one, and a Persian.

Here, at the end of his writings, Isaiah paints a picture of a place where all will be right and nothing good will ever end.

He looked around his surroundings and saw an empire about to crumble. He watched the Assyrians' attack barely averted, but the Babylonians were about to conquer his great city. He knew death and destruction. He foresaw a foreign king (Cyrus) who would make headway into freeing his people.

And then he looked out farther, and he saw recreation, restoration, redemption, and renewal. Re-re-re-re.

Isaiah tells us about the new heavens and the new earth. Isaiah preaches to us about it here, but it's not easy for us to imagine. It's a little bit like explaining Youtube to Abraham Lincoln. Perhaps you can remember living in the world with no concept of the internet, email, cell phones, TikTok, or flying cars.

How can we fully understand what the future will hold?

Let's at least try.

Isaiah made this attempt over two thousand years ago, and we've made advances since then. But he may be able to teach us more than we think he could.

The Problem

Julie and I (Doug) read *Tales of the Kingdom* to our kids. It's a collection of stories analogies to faith and life. In the stories, the knights/rangers often hail each other in two ways. When they are collected and ready to give reports, they are asked, "How goes it in the world?" and they answer, "It doesn't go well. But the king is coming!"

Why is it not going well? Isaiah cries out to God in chapters 63 and 64. He's asking for God to come down and show himself. He wants help.

He's honest about how things are and why the people need God's help. They've wandered from his ways and hardened their hearts (Isa. 63:17). They even blame God for that. Isaiah says: *"Behold, you were angry, and we sinned"* (Isa. 64:5).

He writes:

> *We have all become like one who is unclean, and all of our righteous deeds are like a polluted garment. We all fade like a leaf, and our iniquities, like the wind, take us away. There is no one who calls upon your name, who rouses himself to take hold of you.* (Isa. 64:6–7)

Isaiah starts off with a general "We've sinned," and then he uses metaphors to describe what that looks and feels like. It's like leprosy because it's highly contagious, and it cuts us off from people and community. It's like unclean, polluted garments, like a trash can filled in the bathroom by the toilet, smelling like a pile of dirty soiled diapers and feminine products. It looks like a leaf blowing down the alley with the wind, free to do nothing, without any substance or import. It's apathy, sleeping all day for nothing important to ever happen.

God has let that happen. It's a hell on Earth for him to stop intervening. They've gotten what they thought they wanted, and it's meaningless, a chasing after the wind. He writes:

> *Your holy cities have become a wilderness; Zion has become a wilderness, Jerusalem a desolation. Our holy and beautiful house, where our fathers praised you, has been burned by fire, and all our pleasant places have become ruins.* (Isa. 64:10–11)

Will God keep silent?

It doesn't go well. Will the king come?

Isaiah keeps going.

Things are bad in the midst of God's people. We're not talking about Babylonians or Assyrians. We're talking about the Old Testament church. We are a rebellious people, walking in bad ways, following our own devices. Like in the time of Judges, we do what is right in our own eyes.

We provoke God constantly with our sins, and it's not anti-religious. It's all very religious, sacrificing in gardens, making offerings on bricks and mountains, sitting in tombs and secret places. It's an insult to God for his people to act this way.

We worship our bodies, kids, bank accounts, freedom, lack of commitment, advancement, social status, or our intellect. We sacrifice things all the time. It's all religious, serving the gods and idols we think will make us happy. We're devoted to laws and rules (Whole 30, decluttering, cover your mouth when you sneeze, early to bed and early to rise makes a man healthy wealthy and wise, don't talk to strangers, always leave a one-urinal buffer zone). We seldom stop to think if our rule-following will help our world be better. We assume it will, because well, it's the rule, and we'll worship something if someone tells us what to do.

Isaiah has assessed his people, and thus he's assessed us.

Can you sense any leprosy on you, or are you perfectly spiritually healthy? Got any polluted parts you don't want anyone to notice? Have you had anything float around like dust in the wind?

Are you a sinner?

How disappointed are you? What do you see around you? Your project didn't go well. Your relationship is on the rocks, or you don't have one. You put on fifteen pounds this year. You aren't as good at something as you thought you were. You're depressed or swamped in debt. Your parents are dying or your children have wandered from the church. You just got fired. You're irritable. Your wife doesn't like you right now. You're in a rut. You put your foot in your mouth. You handled a situation poorly.

What will you do with life in this world? Ignore it? Deny it?

And then there's this other problem—all good things must come to an end. I loved my ten years as the RUF campus minister at OU, but I remember my last semester, month, and week. The same is true at City Pres. It will happen with Matt at Shawnee Pres. We're not going to be here forever.

I remember my fortieth birthday party and how fun it was to have everyone there dancing and talking. I brewed two hundred bottles of beer for that party. We sang hymns and danced. Then it was over. We had to clean up and go home.

That happened at my forty-fifth party too. Adam and Kizzie played their last song, and I was sad. My fiftieth took place during the pandemic, and we made the best of it. Then it was over.

I remember our family vacations, important moments, conversations, and our most cherished joys. But they're gone. Vacations end and so do lives.

The Cardinals won the World Series, but that was in 2011. Since then the Cubs have won which is hard to believe.

The Sooners haven't won a football championship since 2000, and that is too long of a drought. They've been close, but they can't seem to seal the deal.

My friend Natalie put it this way when she was talking about beauty: "There is a problem with pretty. That problem is that you can never be pretty enough." So true. You can be pretty today, but what about tomorrow?

It's a messy world out there, even when we get the things we want. Things are disappointing, from first world problems like vacations ending, to the universal ways humans have suffered from the very beginning. People are hungry, impoverished, and dying. Might seems to lead to right. We witness injustice all over the world, nearly every week. Even when we do get what we want, it's over so quickly. That night alone? Time is ticking, and it will end.

Isaiah is realistic about life. Are you as realistic, or are you burying your head in the sand and pretending we're all fine? We've got a problem!

Restoration

Isaiah hasn't shrunk back from this truth. Things are not as they were meant to be. There was creation, and it was good. There was a real fall, and things have degenerated, fallen apart, and broken up. They are contaminated. The good we see is fleeting, and we can't seem to hold onto it at all.

There are people in the world who think the Holocaust never happened. They deny it. They prop up a fantasy world.

There are people who deny racism exists in America today. They think we should stop talking about it, claiming it's just a media sensation.

There are people who refuse to admit their own problems, and they blame everyone else. They look at the world through rose-colored glasses, or they blame everyone else for what's going on with their lives. They won't get help.

Isaiah, however, is not one of these people. He cries out, pleads with God, and he begs for mercy. He intercedes for his people and his place.

Isaiah 64 starts this way:

> Oh that you would rend the heavens and come down, that the mountains might quake at your presence—as when fire kindles brushwood and the fire causes water to boil—to make your name known to your adversaries, and that the nations might tremble at your presence! When you did awesome things that we did not look for, you came down, the mountains quaked at your presence. (Isa. 64:1–3)

Isaiah is crying out to God to come down and work in his midst. He wants God to manifest himself like he has before. He prays for God to change his situation.

He's ready for God to work. He knows his place as a prophet sinner in the midst of sinners. He writes:

> But now, O Lord, you are our Father; we are the clay, and you are the potter; we are all the work of your hand. Be not so terribly angry, O Lord, and remember not iniquity forever. Behold, please look, we are all your people. (Isa. 64:9–10)

"It doesn't go well. But the king is coming!" King, please come, please come, please come. We need your help!

So the question is—what will God do? Will he come?

We often think his delay is his indifference to human suffering and pain. But God answers this entirely differently. In Isaiah 65, he writes:

> I was ready to be sought by those who did not ask for me; I was ready to be found by those who did not seek me. I said, "Here am I, here am I" to a nation that was not called by my name. I spread out my hands all the day to a rebellious people,

who walk in a way that is not good, following their own devices; a people who
provoke me to my face continually. (Isa. 65:1–3)

God says he shows up in the midst of the riot, in the middle of
the pity party, in the center of the cluster. He's calling those who
have blocked him. He's Ubering people who throw up in his car. He's
throwing parties for crashers. He's picking up the tab for those
who've stiffed him and given him bad reviews. He's patient with
smart, F students. He's clothing the naked, feeding the hungry, and
employing the homeless. He spreads out his hands even when he's
spit on and given diseases. He's provoked, but he doesn't take the
bait. He's patient, kind, long suffering, and gracious.

He could throw out the whole batch, but he waits and picks out
the good from the bad grapes so he can make his wine. He reclaims
families from Jacob and Judah, re-pastures flocks, and repopulates
barren lands and people. He feeds his servants and gives them
enough to quench their thirst. His servants rejoice instead of being
put to shame. His people sing for joy. He blesses instead of curses.
He forgets sin and hides it from his eyes.

So we're talking about a personal salvation here. We need a Savior
King Redeemer. We need God to forgive us. We need grace by faith
alone. We need Jesus!

The good news is we have him. He came. He listened. He has
opened our ears and eyes and hearts, or he will. He cares, and he's
come down close. The king has come, and he will return. He's not
left you alone to your own hell forever. He's come in as a Rescuer
who redeems the broken. He's healed the sick, released the captives,
set the prisoners free, cleaned up the dirty, clothed the naked, and fed
the hungry.

But that's not all. He has something even more, better, and
grander. There is something else, something more.

Isaiah paints the picture of restoration for us starting in Isaiah 65:

"For behold, I create new heavens and a new earth, and the former things shall
not be remembered or come into mind. But be glad and rejoice forever in that
which I create; for behold, I create Jerusalem to be a joy, and her people to be a
gladness. I will rejoice in Jerusalem and be glad in my people; no more shall be

heard in it the sound of weeping and the cry of distress. No more shall there be in it an infant who lives but a few days, or an old man who does not fill out his days, for the young man shall die a hundred years old, and the sinner a hundred years old shall be accursed. They shall build houses and inhabit them; they shall plant vineyards and eat their fruit. They shall not build and another inhabit; they shall not plant and another eat; for like the days of a tree shall the days of my people be, and my chosen shall long enjoy the work of their hands. They shall not labor in vain or bear children for calamity, for they shall be the offspring of the blessed of the Lord, and their descendants with them. Before they call I will answer; while they are yet speaking I will hear. The wolf and the lamb shall graze together; the lion shall eat straw like the ox, and dust shall be the serpent's food. They shall not hurt or destroy in all my holy mountain," says the Lord. (Isa. 65:17–25)

God will be about the work of recreating his creation. Not only will it be physically restored, but every aspect of it will be redeemed and renewed, even our emotions and memories, and there will be no more pain. This restored community won't be completely rural or suburban or backwoods, if that is what you think. It also won't be just you and Jesus.

The future looks like a great city, the New Jerusalem. It will bustle with life, activity, skyscrapers, and culture. In this new city, there won't be any sense of what we now experience as spiritual schizophrenia. God will completely know his people, and we will completely know him. Not only will there be no crying or sorrow, but also there won't be anything to cause that sort of pain.

Death won't reign any more. Right now, death cuts off life. Not so in the New Restored City. We saw the death of death foretold in Isaiah 25:7–8: *"And he will swallow up death forever...."* Now we read about growing children instead of death, about long lives.

Isaiah tells a story to make his point. Even if it were possible to have a stowaway sinner in the new heavens and new earth, he would not be able to last. The curse upon sin would reach him and destroy him. There will be no place for death and sin here. When Isaiah says it will be like you live to be a hundred, he actually means you won't die at all. One hundred years old was an impossibly long life in 700 BC.

Then look at what we read about. Houses and vineyards. What do you think will be happening in the new heavens and the new earth? Many of us have been taught we will be floating around on the clouds with harps in our hands, singing and worshiping all day long. We may be worshiping, but not as you think. We'll be worshiping in our houses, and brewing wine while we work. Nothing we do will be frustrated, yet we will still have work to do. Isn't that interesting? In the end we'll have one commandment to follow: *"Be glad and rejoice forever in that which I create."*

So what we're saying is sort of a paradox. The new creations will be new and not new. If you take out sin and death and disease and rebellion, wouldn't that be so radical it's difficult to even imagine or talk about? That is the way in which it is new. But new creations will not be new in the sense that you will be you, I will be me, and we will have a history and society and *this earth*. Sin and death will be something we try to remember. We won't be married. We'll be perfectly united, and all will be made right. All must be well.

We won't have to worry about prisons, capital punishment, divorce law, police officers, loan sharks, corrupt officials, increased taxes, bad words, smart bombs, runaway technology, sexual abuse, power plays, manipulation, unhealthy enmeshed families, or child welfare. That world is old. This one is made new.

God is restoring everything to its original, good intent. We're not set back into the Garden of Eden because the garden has become a dense, populated, just, beautiful city. Grace makes things right.

Isaiah finishes up this part of the picture with ideas of oneness— with the Lord as he anticipates our needs and our now-lack of hope-lessness and desperation. It's a oneness with his voice, his desires, and our actions. He unites us with creation in a harmony without the curse of death on us.

Notice Isaiah mentions that *"dust shall be on the serpent's food."* What is he thinking of? Why would he mention that?

Surely he is thinking of the great enemy of God's creation, the serpent depicted in Genesis 3:14. And what do we find in the new creation? The curse upon sin still stands. We don't make peace with sin and death. It is still and always will be wrong, evil and condemned. Our God is the Holy God and always will be.

Isn't this what we all want and what we're all hoping for? A better place and restored creation where everything is right, and nothing is wrong.

When our kids were young, I was convicted of trying to do a better job of leading my family as we went out into the world. Instead of just trudging dutifully off to school and then coming back, I've tried to be more intentional about what it was we were doing as we were going to learn and work in the world. Dietrich Bonhoeffer challenged me about this in his book about community.

So we got up, got ready, ate breakfast, and we assembled at 8am sharp in the kitchen, all ready to go. Then I read a psalm and prayed, asking God to help us as we learned and worked and honored him in all we said and did. We sang a few verses of a hymn so we could learn the hymns we sang at church and the kids would know them by heart.

And at the end of our time, I added a last part. I cried out, and then they repeated "To the King! To the Restoration!"

I'm not saying that was a resounding success, but we did it. You can ask them if they remember. I do. It mattered to me at least. They didn't give it the full vigor it deserved. But it should be our battle cry to go out into the world. The king is coming. He's restoring his world.

Worship

Isaiah next reminds us it will be God's worshipers who are there when this new creation is fully ushered in. Will you be in the number? Chapter 66 starts off with something we've heard before. He talks about God's transcendence and his holiness. He writes:

> Heaven is my throne, and the earth is my footstool; what is the house that you build for me, and what is the place of my rest? All these things my hand has made, and so all of these things came to be. (Isa. 66:1–2)

God is saying, "You made the temple, a wall, and an infrastructure? That's like making a slushee at Sonic. Anyone can be taught to do it." God is not impressed. He made the universe!

If God is transcendent, magnificent, and so out there, then how do we have any hope of a relationship with him?

He tells us he will and can relate to some, and he describes the characteristics of that group of people. At the end of Isaiah 66:2, we read, *"But this is the one to whom I will look: he who is humble and contrite in spirit and trembles at my word...."*

He looks at the humble. One commentator writes, "The humble are, socially, those who are at the bottom of life's heap, dominated by stronger forces and interests; religiously, they are those who willingly take the lowest place before God."[1] They're not proud. They're not arrogant. They're not full of themselves. They know they need grace, mercy, and help. They know they don't know everything.

He looks at the contrite. The contrite are the "disabled, here used with spiritual significance: one who is aware of the damage wrought by sin, of personal inability to stand upright before God."[2] The contrite are repentant. They regularly ask for forgiveness. They rarely defend their positions, and they learn from others.

And he looks at the one who trembles at his word. "'Trembles' speaks of a sensitive, concerned longing to please."[3] They want to know God's Word. They look for God in the Scriptures and cry out to hear his voice. They show up to learn, and they're thankful for any chance they have to sit underneath gracious Bible teaching about Jesus.

Who models that for you? We may have heroes in sports or film or finance or community involvement. Who do you know that truly exemplifies Isaiah 66:2?

I remember attending a Celebration Service for my friend Rev. Chris Garriott. He had been the youth pastor at Heritage Presbyterian Church for eight years and was moving to Maryland to be the RUF Campus Minister there. Chris and I went through our ordination exams together, standing side by side answering questions before the assembled elders (he received easier questions than I did).

The Celebration Service was a wonderful time of singing hymns and praying for Chris.

My friend Chris Garriott is humble and contrite in spirit. He is self-effacing, kind, compassionate, looks out for others, a servant, and he is a man of God. He is what Isaiah 66:2 is talking about. And at the service, the pastor gave him a charge from 2 Timothy 3 and 4, reminding him he has been called by the Church and by God to preach the Word.

There are many temptations to do anything but preach the word. It honestly doesn't feel that effective sometimes. You look around and see other churches and ministries who don't preach the Bible, and they have ten times the number of people. But we must remain faithful to our calling to preach the what God has said.

And if we preach, God's people must remain faithful to their calling to listen. To, as Isaiah puts it, tremble at the Word both read and preached.

Paul commended the believers in Thessalonica this way:

> *And we also thank God constantly for this, that when you received the word of God, which you heard from us, you accepted it not as the word of men but as what it really is, the word of God, which is at work in you believers.* (2 Thess. 2:13)

Is that you? Is that me? Is that our modern, American church? Are we humble, contrite in spirit, and trembling at his word? What would it mean to be like that?

We're worshipers of Jesus. It's not all about us. It's about him. Let's be true worshipers. Isaiah decries false worship, whether it be traditional or liberal or conservative or contemporary.

I read a New York Times article about a study of lyrics that was done recently.[4] Dr. Nathan DeWall studied lyrics from 1980 to 2007 and found the hit songs of the 80s focused on happiness and togetherness. Ebony and Ivory living together in perfect harmony. Kool and the Gang sang let's all celebrate and have a good time. Diana Ross and Lionel Richie sang of two hearts that beat as one. John Lennon sang of our life together.

And now? Justin Timberlake says he's bringing sexy back.

Beyonce says she's blazin,' and you watch her with amazement.
Fergie says she needs personal time alone.
It's personal. Me, myself, and I.
Everything points toward the personal and not the communal.
That's true in our modern worship songs too. Haven't you noticed?
Over and over in praise songs people sing about me, me, me. What I
want. What I feel.

Our songs in church worship should break us out of our personal
idolatry and our focus on ourselves. To remind ourselves, we sing in
a community of people—past, present and future. And we're not
singing love songs about ourselves, but about our great God. He is
the one who is the focus, not us.

We are needy but confident. We are humble but assured in his
love for us. We should focus on him.

There is a reminder in Isaiah 66 that God will not stand for
pretenders in his midst. He hates it when people claim the form of
worship but do not have the love of God in their hearts. There is
coming a day of perfect intimacy where all will be set right.

That is the message of the kingdom. To some, it sounds like sure
and utter death. But to those whom he has called, it sounds like life
and peace. And he assures us it is possible because he is able to do it
—abundantly. He likens it to painless childbirth(!) and to a whole
litter of children. As these children grow, they are able to nurse in
satisfaction and abundance.

I remember watching Julie nurse our children and thinking how
both strange and wonderful it was. I had no experience with this, no
way to relate to it, and yet I felt a joy in watching the natural aspects
of how it all worked, of how God designed her body to meet our children's needs. I marveled at the emotional connection I could see.
What a bond between mother and child! It may be sort of uncomfort-
able, but one of the pictures of assurance we get is that we will drink
deeply with delight from God's glorious breast.

Whoa. This would have been a beautiful picture to an ancient
culture, much more so than ours where we feel squeamish about this
topic. It is natural, and it is good.

God describes himself as a mother. He pictures the Church effortlessly bearing children. What a strange metaphor, but it's a natural one.

Isaiah finishes this idea of worship in the new creation with peace, hope, and joy. He says he will comfort us like a mother comforts her children. He will do that in the new Jerusalem. There will be peace like a river extending your way. You will see, and you shall experience in a way that cannot be taken away. You will see, and your heart will rejoice. You will flourish.

You know those moments when everything comes together, just for a second, maybe?

Listening to the symphony. Hearing the beautiful sounds intermingle with perfection.

Sitting on the edge of the Grand Canyon. All is well. This is good. God's creation is both enormous and relational.

Finishing a job well done.

Holding his hand on a walk.

Taking the Lord's Supper at church.

Turning the last page of a great novel.

Acing a test.

Sipping your coffee on the porch.

Laughing with friends.

Winning a game of Settlers.

But that feeling never lasts does it? It either ends too fast or slowly starts to deteriorate. You have to go home from vacation. The coffee gets acidic and cold. You lose the next game of Settlers. Your friend moves away. You have another test next week. Why is it so hard to get at that "thing"? Maybe because the thing isn't here at all but resides somewhere else.

As C. S. Lewis so aptly writes:

> If I find myself a desire which no experience in this world can satisfy, the most probable explanation is that I was made for another world. If none of my earthly pleasures can satisfy it, that does not prove that the universe is a fraud. Probably earthly pleasures were never meant to satisfy it, but only to arouse it, to suggest the real thing.... I must make it the main object of life to press on to that other country and to help others do the same.[5]

Those moments will continue forever. Your bones will flourish. You will have peace. It will never be taken away by his enemies. To the King, to the Restoration!

The Restoration

Ah, but remember this—those moments will come to those whom the Lord loves. And those are the humble, the contrite in spirit, those who tremble at his word. Did you forget? Are you one of these?

To the rest—to the proud, the arrogant and the self-sufficient—he won't appear like a comforting mother.

He will come in fire. He will come with chariots, weapons of destruction. He will come in anger, fury, and rebuke. He will come in judgment, with the sword. And here is the chilling end of his jealousy: *"And those slain by the Lord shall be many."*

Friends, I have to remind you of something. It's my duty. The good news only comes in the context of the bad news.

—There is a judgment coming. It may come today. It may come tomorrow or tonight. I do not know when or how, but it will come.

There will be a final payment. This has to be true, and you know it does. If God is truly right, good, and holy, then wrong has to be paid for. It cannot be swept under the rug. God is good, yes. He is gracious to be sure. He is merciful and long suffering. But he is not stupid, nor is he unjust, nor is he going to wink at sin. We are sinners at the hands of an angry God.

The truth is wrong must be held accountable. You can pay for it, or you can acknowledge your wrong and need, cry out to him, and have your sin paid for by this Suffering Servant in Isaiah, by Jesus Christ.

God has sent a sign. The cross was the epitome of an excruciating death. However, now the cross is a sign of victory over death. It is the image of a torture device that you wear around your neck, and we hang in our buildings. But it's transformed by Jesus and now a sign of the death of death, given partially when Jesus raised from the tomb on Easter morning and fully coming one day soon.

That is what we look to. People from all nations, little and big, prominent and obscure, who have seen the sign—they are coming. Missionaries are bringing their friends and families to worship the King of Kings and Lord of Lords. They come on all means of transportation (even dromedaries). They come as gifts to God. They come safely to the holy mountain of the Lord.

We see a new creation, a new city, a new society, and we are coming to a new house. What will we do there? We will worship! We will enjoy acceptance in Jerusalem and constant communion with the Lord. We need to cheer on and cheer for the church as we move toward this day.

It is a glorious vision, but it has a sobering end.

In the midst of this great city, there is a cemetery. When all have gathered, they make a point of going out to look at the fate from which they have been delivered. Motyer writes:

> They enjoy the day of salvation, but they do not allow themselves to forget the day of vengeance…. The accusation leveled and made out against them is that they rebelled: they knew the word of the Lord but deliberately and willfully went their own way.[6]

The people don't go out there to gloat, for it is far too awful for that. They go to see again the wages of sin and the fruit of rebellion and thereby to be motivated to obedience and love of the Word of God.[7]

Do you realize that you deserve hell? Are you angry at God? Are you offended that he allows a fallen world? Then you don't understand yourself and your part in this tragedy. You're missing it. Do you think God is keeping people in hell who don't want to be there? More accurately, hell is eternal souls who don't want God and who are getting their way. Hell is what people want. They want an eternity without God, so they get it. They never wanted God in their lives, and he obliges them.

We all deserve this, and in one sense we all get it. Someone is going to pay for your sins. It will either be you, or it will be Jesus Christ, who died in the place of sinners. He got what you deserve so you can get what he deserved. He took what you owe, so you can get what he earned.

Do you see God has done something about it after all? It may not have been what you expected, but he is God, and you are not.

God himself came down into this world and suffered hell out of the love, to save us from our folly. It's time for us to humble ourselves. It's time to change the subject in our minds from blaming God for ruining the world to owning our real moral guilt before him, so that we can receive his saving love in Jesus Christ.[8]

In other words, heaven is eternal souls who long for God, and they are getting all they want and more. They're getting God himself in infinite, eternal measure.[9]

At the very end of the Bible in the book of Revelation, we get a vision for the city where we're headed.

Things are headed to end in the city of God, the city of Zion. As we sing "Glorious things of thee are spoken, Zion city of our God," he'll wipe away every tear, and there won't be any more death. All will be made new. And God will be there.

Why? Because the Lamb of God will be there. The Lamb who takes away the sin of the world. Jesus Christ is that Lamb of God.

All the death and pain was put on him so you could experience hope and joy and freedom. He took the darkness so you could have the light of the world. All sin collapses onto him so your life could expand in greatness in this new city. He was blighted so you could flourish. You deserved hell. God punishes sin. You need that. You need a God who is angry at sin, who hates sin and does something about it. His anger is good.

But he's also loving. He isn't only angry. He loves his children. That love and that anger come together on the cross of Christ, the Lamb of God who was slain for the sins of the world.

That's why you can come to the city of God. We aren't there yet. But it's coming. It's coming someday. We want to see you there. I want to worship with you both now and then. I want the crowds to be pressing in so we can see Jesus together.

There is a place for you, a place without sorrow, a world where pleasure reigns. A land of peace and glory. Do you want to go? In the book of Isaiah, God says, I will take you there. Instead of Isaiah's chapter 6 cry, "Here I am, Lord!," we see throughout the book, God saying, "Here I am! Look! Follow! Trust!"

Are you willing to see him? To come to him?

All you need is your need. He is looking for the humble, the contrite in spirit, those who tremble at his Word. He is bringing a great people to himself and to his new city. Will you be a part of the joyous number?

I do not want to gather at the headstone of your grave in the new city. I will mourn for you and will never see you again. Instead, why don't we fulfill our destinies together as the redeemed community, worshiping God in extreme happiness and contentment? Just think of all the work we'll get done. All the beauty. All the places we'll be able to explore. How it will be to talk and relate to each other without sin. We'll be making the world better and better. I can't wait to be at the best place in the world with you!

It will be truly great and forever great.

God's worshippers are headed there forever, and we have foretastes of that now. Amen!

———

To the King! To the Restoration!

NOTES

Isaiah 1

1. Peter Craigie, *The Book of Deuteronomy*, The New International Commentary of the Old Testament (Grand Rapids: Eerdmans, 1976), 263.
2. Patrick Fairbairn, *Prophecy: Viewed in Respect to Its Distinctive Nature, Special function, and Proper Interpretation*, second ed. (Edinburgh: T. and T. Clark, 1865), 4.
3. John C. Collins, "Prophet's" (lecture, Covenant Seminary, St. Louis, MO, late 1990s).
4. J. Alec Motyer, *Isaiah*, Tyndale Old Testament Commentaries, reprint ed. (InterVarsity Press: Downers Grove, 2009), 34
5. This summary has been edited from Kevin Twit's sermon notes.
6. James Baldwin, "As Much Truth As One Can Bear" in *The New York Times Book Review* (14 January 1962); republished in *The Cross of Redemption: Uncollected Writings* (2011), edited by Randall Kenan.
7. William Cowper, "Sometimes a Light Surprises," (1779), https://hymnary.org/text/sometimes_a_light_surprises.

Isaiah 6

1. John N. Oswalt, *The Book of Isaiah, Chapters 1–39*, The New International Commentary of the New Testament (Eerdmans Publishing: Grand Rapids, 1986), 177.
2. Oswalt, *The Book of Isaiah, Chapters 1–39*, 178.
3. Annie Dillard, *Pilgrim at Tinker Creek*, (Harper Perennial Modern Classics: New York, 2013).
4. Barry G. Webb, *The Message of Isaiah*, Bible Speaks Today (IVP Academic: Downers Grove, 1997), 59.
5. Motyer, *Isaiah*, 71.
6. This illustration comes from Timothy Keller (and he says he got it from Jonathan Edwards).
7. This illustration comes from Tim Keller.
8. On the day I wrote this chapter, I did pilates for the first time. I was next to two women, both in their 60s or 70s. I cannot touch my toes. They were pilates masters. I was in the presence of pilates greatness and was ashamed.
9. Some of these may have happened to me.
10. Webb, *The Message of Isaiah*, 59.
11. Oswalt, *The Book of Isaiah, Chapters 1–39*, 182–183.
12. Oswalt, *The Book of Isaiah, Chapters 1–39*, 183.
13. Webb, *The Message of Isaiah*, 60
14. Motyer, *Isaiah*, 72.
15. Anne Lamott, *Traveling Mercies: Some Thoughts on Faith* (New York: Anchor Books, 1999).
16. Oswalt, *The Book of Isaiah, Chapters 1–39*, 185.
17. Motyer, *Isaiah*, 72.
18. Webb, *The Message of Isaiah*, 60.

19. Oswalt, *The Book of Isaiah, Chapters 1–39*, 186.
20. My friend Josh Spears says he heard this passage taught six times one semester at his Christian college. All were to prompt a missionary zeal. I think that is one possible application, but Isaiah wasn't exactly a missionary, and his message wasn't exactly what I normally hear in churches today.
21. A phrase from Timothy Keller.
22. A phrase from Timothy Keller.
23. Gregory Boyle, *Tattoos on the Heart*, (New York: Free Press, 2011),1.
24. Boyle, *Tattoos on the Heart*, 30.
25. Boyle, *Tattoos on the Heart*, 31.

Isaiah 7, 9, 11

1. from Eugene Peterson's translation in *The Message*
2. Peterson again
3. http://www.bmj.com/content/347/bmj.f7102
4. https://en.wikipedia.org/wiki/Miraculous_births
5. https://en.wikipedia.org/wiki/Miraculous_birthsung junkyard slave, Anakin Skywalker, is discovered by Jedi Master Qui-Gon Jinn and his padawan, Obi Wan Kenobi, who (mainly Qui-Gon) believes him to be the "Chosen One" who is prophesied to bring balance to the Force and destroy the Sith. Qui-Gon Jinn is convinced on this fact when Anakin's mother reveals to him that Anakin has no father and was possibly conceived by the Force itself. This fact explains why Anakin has the highest midi-chlorian count of any lifeform. Also, the coming of the Sith'ari, an ancient Sith prophecy, became somewhat well known in Darth Revan's Sith Empire. The Sith'ari was said to be a perfect (according to the Sith philosophy) being who would rise to power and bring balance to the Force. According to prophecy, the Sith'ari would rise up and destroy the Sith, but in the process would return to lead the Sith and make them stronger than ever before. It is believed that the prophecy of the Sith Sith'ari and the prophecies of the Jedi Chosen One refer to the same individual; namely Anakin Skywalker/Darth Vader, who made the Sith stronger than ever by wiping out the Jedi Knights and assisting Darth Sidious in his rise to power, but then destroyed the Sith when he betrayed and killed Sidious, sacrificing himself in the process, thus fulfilling the ancient prophecy of the Sith'ari.
   From http://en.wikipedia.org/wiki/Messiahs_in_fiction_and_fantasy#Star_Wars
6. Webb, The Message of Isaiah, 68–69.
7. From *Game of Thrones*.
8. From Oswalt, 247–248 and Dr. Collins' notes on this passage
9. I have a nick in one of my baseball caps I was wearing when the chainsaw caught and kicked back. That's not good.
10. https://en.wikipedia.org/wiki/Abraham_Lincoln%27s_second_inaugural_address
11. https://www.youtube.com/watch?v=tU8rmsEiPEU

Isaiah 24-25

1. http://www.cracked.com/blog/the-7-stupidest-things-that-make-people-proud/
2. http://www.huffingtonpost.com/localeur/what-factors-make-a-city-urban-planning_b_5511883.html
3. https://www.planetizen.com/node/15988

Isaiah 26

1. https://www.thisamericanlife.org/radio-archives/episode/342/transcript
2. https://crcvc.ca/docs/A%20Grief%20Like%20No%20Other.pdf
3. https://crcvc.ca/docs/A%20Grief%20Like%20No%20Other.pdffinish-the-dishes-when-im-dead/
4. http://www.workingmother.com/work-life-balance-may-you-rest-in-peace#page-5
5. http://www.workingmother.com/work-life-balance-may-you-rest-in-peace#page-6
6. Yolanda Jones, USA Today Network, April 2, 2017, https://www.commercialappeal.com/story/news/local/2017/04/02/rip-t-shirt-businesses-growing-memphis-families-honor-their-dead/99592846/
7. Ibid.
8. This story was found in the book *All These Wonders*.

Isaiah 40

1. http://www.youtube.com/watch?v=G0FtgZNOD44
2. Illustration from a Discovery Channel show
3. Ortland, 247
4. Deep Thought said that it couldn't come up with the question to which the answer 42 went to for them, but that a program could be built that could come up with the question in 10 million years. The computer's name was Earth. So they decided to have Earth built at the planet factory, Magrathean. And the beings ruled the earth disguised as mice, running the program. They were five minutes from finding out the answer when Earth was destroyed in a bungled accident by the Vogons. Slartibartfast took the hero of the book, Arthur Dent, on a tour of Earth Mark Two.
   "The wall defied the imagination—seduced it and defeated it. The wall was so paralyzingly vast and sheer that its top, bottom and sides passed away beyond the reach of sight. The mere shock of vertigo could kill a man. The wall appeared perfectly flat. It would take the finest laser-measurement equipment to detect that as it climbed, apparently to infinity, as it dropped dizzily away, as it planed out to either side, it also curved. It met itself again thirteen light seconds away. In other words, the wall formed inside of a hollow sphere, a sphere over three million miles across and flooded with unimaginable light. "Welcome," said Slartibartfast... "to the factory floor."..." This is where we make most of our planets."
   Slartibartfast explained about how they were making Earth Mark Two from the blueprints of the first one. He was particularly proud of Norway, since he was an expert on coastlines and took delight in the Norwegian fjords. He'd won an award for that work.
5. This is adapted from Tim Keller. Katie Willis reminds me to not forget the Libertarians.
6. Ortland, 232
7. John N. Oswalt, *The Book of Isaiah, Chapters 40–66*, The New International Commentary of the Old Testament (Eerdmans Publishing: Grand Rapids, 1998), 45.
8. Oswalt,The Book of Isaiah, Chapters 40–66, 45.
9. Ortland, 251
10. Ortland, 236
11. Ortland, 254
12. Which is a line from one of Neitchze's writings of all things
13. Oswalt, 75
14. Oswalt, 74

Isaiah 42–43

1. http://aboutgaoyou.com/history/floods/the_floods.aspx
2. https://exploredia.com/top-10-biggest-fires-in-the-world/
3. This is the second chainsaw reference.
4. Please purchase and read *Through the Valley: How Psalm 23 Helps Us in Suffering*, a book by Rob Wootton.

Isaiah 44

1. Ortland, 289
2. Oswalt, vol. 2, 161
3. Motyer, *Isaiah*, 274.
4. Motyer, *Isaiah* 281.
5. Motyer, *Isaiah* 281.
6. Slightly adapted from Keller
7. from David Powlison, "Idols of the Heart and Vanity Fair"
   http://jamiehart.typepad.com/files/idols-of-the-heart-powlison.pdf

Isaiah 53–54

1. https://en.wikipedia.org/wiki/James_Hogue

Isaiah 55

1. Brueggemann, Westminster John Knox Press; Fourth Impression edition (October 1, 1998)
2. TE Ray Cannata loves hot dogs.

Isaiah 58, 61, 62

1. https://en.wikipedia.org/wiki/Susan_Boyle
2. https://www.lausanne.org/content/manifesto/the-manila-manifesto

Isaiah 63–66

1. Motyer, *Isaiah*, 401.
2. Motyer, *Isaiah*, 401.
3. Motyer, *Isaiah* 401.
4. http://www.nytimes.com/2011/04/26/science/26tier.html?_r=1
5. C. S. Lewis, *Mere Christianity*, 106, (HarperSanFrancisco, 2001)
6. Motyer, *Isaiah*, 407.
7. Motyer, *Isaiah* 408.
8. Oswalt, 456
9. Oswalt, 445

ABOUT WHITE BLACKBIRD BOOKS

White blackbirds are extremely rare, but they are real. They are blackbirds that have turned white over the years as their feathers have come in and out over and over again. They are a redemptive picture of something you would never expect to see but that has slowly come into existence over time.

There is plenty of hurt and brokenness in the world. There is the hopelessness that comes in the midst of lost jobs, lost health, lost homes, lost marriages, lost children, lost parents, lost dreams, loss.

But there also are many white blackbirds. There are healed marriages, children who come home, friends who are reconciled. There are hurts healed, children fostered and adopted, communities restored. Some would call these events entirely natural, but really they are unexpected miracles.

The books in this series are not commentaries, nor are they crammed with unique insights. Rather, they are a collage of biblical truth applied to current times and places. The authors share their poverty and trust the Lord to use their words to strengthen and encourage his people.

May this series help you in your quest to know Christ as he is found in the Gospel through the Scriptures. May you look for and even expect the rare white blackbirds of God's redemption through Christ in your midst. May you be thankful when you look down and see your feathers have turned. May you also rejoice when you see that others have been unexpectedly transformed by Jesus.

ALSO BY WHITE BLACKBIRD BOOKS